COLLECTIONS

IN GOOD COMPANY

Program Authors
Richard L. Allington
Jesús Cortez
Patricia M. Cunningham
Sam Leaton Sebesta
Robert J. Tierney

Program Consultants
Molly S. McLaurin
Robert Slavin
Zena Sutherland

**Instructional
Consultant**
John C. Manning

Critic Readers
Karen Babb
Donald McFeely

Pupil Readers
Britta Keller Arendt
Gena Avery
DeLeah Regina Blake
Christopher D. Littlefield
Tom McMillon
Christina Patiño
Jason Akil´ Patterson
Stephanie Santillan
Steven Tom

**Scott, Foresman
and Company**

Editorial Office:
Glenview, Illinois

Regional Offices:
Sunnyvale, California
Tucker, Georgia
Glenview, Illinois
Oakland, New Jersey
Carrollton, Texas

Acknowledgments

Text
Page 12: "Another Big Event" (pp. 160-182) from *Ramona Forever* by Beverly Cleary. Illustrated by Alan Tiegreen. Copyright © 1984 by Beverly Cleary. Illustration © 1984 by William Morrow & Company. Reprinted by permission of William Morrow & Company and Julia MacRae Books.
Page 35: From "Beverly Cleary" by David Reuther, *The Horn Book*, August 1984, Vol. LX, No. 4, p. 440. Copyright © 1984 by The Horn Book, Inc. Reprinted by permission.
Page 37: "Some Things Don't Make Any Sense At All" from *If I Were In Charge of the World and Other Worries* by Judith Viorst. Copyright © 1981 Judith Viorst. Reprinted with the permission of Atheneum Publishers, a division of Macmillan, Inc., Lescher & Lescher, Ltd. and A. M. Heath & Co., Ltd.
Page 46: *Anna, Grandpa, and the Big Storm* by Carla Stevens. Copyright © 1982 by Carla Stevens. Illustrations © 1982 by Margot Tomes. Reprinted by permission of Clarion Books/Ticknor & Fields, a Houghton Mifflin Company and Penguin Books Ltd.
Page 89: "Winter" by Dorothy Aldis. Reprinted by permission of G. P. Putnam's Sons from *Everything and Anything* by Dorothy Aldis, copyright 1925-1927, copyright renewed 1953-1955 by Dorothy Aldis.
Page 98: From *A Grain of Wheat: A Writer Begins* by Clyde Robert Bulla. Copyright © 1985 by Clyde Robert Bulla. Reprinted by permission of David R. Godine, Publisher, Inc.
Page 131: "Thinking" from *At the Top of My Voice and Other Poems* by Felice Holman. Text copyright © 1970 by Felice Holman. Reprinted by permission of the author.
Page 140: *Thumbeline* by Hans Christian Andersen, translated by Anthea Bell, illustrated by Lisbeth Zwerger. Copyright © 1985, English text, Neugebauer Press USA Inc. Reprinted by permission of Picture Book Studio USA.
Page 170: "The World Is Big, The World Is Small" by Ella Jenkins. Copyright © 1966 by River Bend Music Inc. and assigned to Ella Jenkins. Published by Oak Publications. All Rights Reserved. Used by permission.
Page 180: "My Very Strange Teeth" from *The Stories Julian Tells* by Ann Cameron, illustrated by Ann Strugnell. Copyright © 1981 by Ann Cameron. Copyright © 1981 by Ann Strugnell. Reprinted by permission of Pantheon Books, a Division of Random House, Inc., Ann Cameron and Curtis Brown, Ltd.
Page 188: "Gloria Who Might Be My Best Friend" from *The Stories Julian Tells* by Ann Cameron, illustrated by Ann Strugnell. Copyright © 1981 by Ann Cameron. Copyright © 1981 by Ann Strugnell. Reprinted by permission of Pantheon Books, a Division of Random House, Inc., Ann Cameron and Curtis Brown, Ltd.
Page 196: "The Bet" from *More Stories Julian Tells* by Ann Cameron, illustrated by Ann Strugnell. Copyright © 1986 by Ann Cameron. Copyright © 1986 by Ann Strugnell. Reprinted by permission of Alfred A. Knopf, Inc. and Victor Gollancz Ltd.

Page 205: "poem for rodney" from *Spin a Soft Black Song* by Nikki Giovanni. Copyright © 1971, 1985 by Nikki Giovanni. Reprinted by permission of Farrar, Straus and Giroux, Inc.
Page 214: *The Rooster Who Understood Japanese* by Yoshiko Uchida. Text copyright © 1976 by Yoshiko Uchida. Reprinted by permission.
Page 239: "Rooster Rhyme" from *Chinese Mother Goose Rhymes* selected and edited by Robert Wyndham. Copyright © 1968 by Robert Wyndham. Reprinted by permission of Philomel Books.
Page 248: From *Amigo* by Byrd Baylor Schweitzer and illustrated by Garth Williams. Text copyright © 1963 Byrd Baylor Schweitzer. Illustrations copyright © 1963 Garth Williams. Reprinted by permission of Macmillan Publishing Company and Byrd Baylor Schweitzer.
Page 279: "Chums" from *Laughing Muse* by Arthur Guiterman. Copyright 1915 by Arthur Guiterman. Reprinted by permission of Louise H. Sclove.
Page 288: From *Peter and the Wolf* by Serge Prokofieff, illustrated by Warren Chappell. Text published in 1940 by Alfred A. Knopf, Inc. Illustrations copyright 1940 and renewed 1968 by Alfred A. Knopf, Inc. Reprinted by permission of Alfred A. Knopf, Inc.
Page 310: Edited version of *Oh, A-Hunting We Will Go* by John Langstaff and illustrated by Nancy Winslow Parker is printed by permission of Margaret K. McElderry Books, Macmillan Publishing Company, John Langstaff and Nancy Winslow Parker. Text copyright © 1974 by John Langstaff. Illustrations copyright © 1974 by Nancy Winslow Parker.
Page 312: Excerpt from *The Sign on Rosie's Door* by Maurice Sendak, text and illustrations. Copyright © 1960 by Maurice Sendak. Reprinted by permission of Harper & Row, Publishers, Inc. and The Bodley Head.
Page 320: Reprinted from *Behind the Scenes of a Broadway Musical*. Copyright © 1982 by Bill Powers. Used by permission of Crown Publishers, Inc.

Acknowledgments continued on page 480

ISBN 0–673–73353–X

When I was ten years old, I wrote my first stories on booklets made of brown wrapping paper. I also started a "Journal of Special Events." Whenever something special happened—like getting my first dog—I held on to the magic of that moment by writing about it in my journal. I saved many magic moments that way—some happy, some sad. I think that's what books and writing are all about.

I hope you will discover many magic moments about all kinds of people and places by reading as many stories and books as you can. Happy reading!

Yoshiko Uchida

Award-winning author Yoshiko Uchida wrote *The Rooster Who Understood Japanese*, which appears on page 211.

Contents

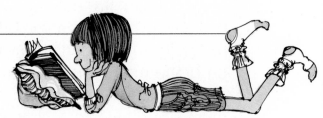

Ramona Forever

by Beverly Cleary

Illustrated by
Alan Tiegreen

Introducing

Do grown-ups ever tell you how big you're getting and then call you a "little" boy or girl? Do you ever feel that being eight years old is an in-between age to be? Ramona Quimby, age eight, often feels that way in *Ramona Forever.* Now that the Quimby family is expecting a new baby, she wonders where she will fit in. Ramona is used to having an older sister, Beezus. Now, though, she won't be the baby of the family anymore.

The Next Big Event
What a year this has been for the Quimbys! Months ago, Ramona and Beezus buried the family cat, Picky-picky, when he suddenly died. After that, Ramona's dad got a new job as manager of the Shop-rite Market. The latest big event was Aunt Bea and Uncle Hobart's wedding.

It's time for another big event. The newest Quimby is due to be born. Somehow, the Quimbys are sure it will be a boy. They have decided that Algernon, or Algie, for short, is a good name for the new baby. Ramona's mom is ready. She's had a suitcase packed to take to the hospital for weeks.

Getting to Know Ramona

In *Ramona Forever,* the author Beverly Cleary shows you what Ramona is like by what Ramona says. Ramona's words tell you how she feels about her family and everything that happens to her.

As you're reading this part of the book on your own, find out how Ramona feels about the new baby in her family.

Aunt Bea and Uncle Hobart's wedding is over. The newlyweds are on their way to Alaska with Ramona's and Beezus's white shoes dangling from the truck's bumper for good luck. The wedding was a happy event for Ramona. Will the arrival of baby Algie be as happy?

Another Big Event

After the wedding, everyone felt let down, the way they always felt the day after Christmas, only worse. Nothing seemed interesting after so much excitement. Grandpa Day had flown back to his sunshine and shuffleboard. Mr. Quimby was at work all day. Friends had gone off to camp, to the mountains, or the beach. Howie and Willa Jean had gone to visit their other grandmother.

"Girls, please stop moping around," said Mrs. Quimby.

"We can't find anything to do," said Beezus.

Ramona was silent. If she complained, her mother would tell her to clean out her closet.

"Read a book," said Mrs. Quimby. "Both of you, read a book."

"I've read all my books a million times," said Ramona, who usually enjoyed rereading her favorites.

"Then go to the library." Mrs. Quimby was beginning to sound irritable.

"It's too hot," complained Ramona.

Mrs. Quimby glanced at her watch.

"Mother, are you expecting someone?" asked Ramona. "You keep looking at your watch."

"I certainly am," said her mother. "A stranger." With a big sigh, Mrs. Quimby sank heavily to the couch, glanced at her watch again, and closed her eyes. The girls exchanged guilty looks. Their poor mother, worn out by Algie kicking her when there was so much of her to feel hot.

"Mother, are you all right?" Beezus sounded worried.

"I'm fine," snapped Mrs. Quimby, which surprised the girls into behaving.

That evening, the sisters helped their mother put together a cold supper of tuna fish salad and sliced tomatoes. While the family was eating, Mr. Quimby told them that now that the "Hawaiian Holidays" sale with bargains in fresh pineapple and papaya had come to an end, all the Shop-rite markets were preparing for "Western Bar-b-q Week" with specials on steak, baked beans, tomato sauce, and chili. He planned to paint bucking broncos on the front windows.

Mrs. Quimby nibbled at her salad and glanced at her watch.

"And everybody will see your paintings," said Ramona, happy that her father was now an artist as well as a market manager.

"Not quite the same as an exhibit in a museum," said Mr. Quimby, who did not sound as happy as Ramona expected.

Mrs. Quimby pushed her chair farther from the table and glanced at her watch. All eyes were on her.

"Shall I call the doctor?" asked Mr. Quimby.

"Please," said Mrs. Quimby as she rose from the table, hugged Algie, and breathed, "Oo-oo."

Ramona and Beezus, excited and frightened, looked at one another. At last! The fifth Quimby would soon be here. Nothing would be the same again, ever. Mr. Quimby reported that the doctor would meet them at the hospital. Without being asked, Beezus ran for the bag her mother had packed several weeks ago.

Mrs. Quimby kissed her daughters. "Don't look so frightened," she said. "Everything is going to be all right. Be good girls, and Daddy will be home as soon as he can." She bent forward and hugged Algie again.

The house suddenly seemed empty. The girls listened to the car back out of the driveway. The sound of the motor became lost in traffic.

"Well," said Beezus, "I suppose we might as well do the dishes."

"I suppose so." Ramona tested all the doors, including the door to the basement, to make sure they were locked.

"Too bad Picky-picky isn't here to eat all this tuna salad no one felt like eating." Beezus scraped the plates into the garbage.

To her own surprise, Ramona burst into tears and buried her face in a dish towel. "I just want Mother to come home," she wept.

Beezus wiped her soapy hands on the seat of her cutoff jeans. Then she put her arms around Ramona, something she had never done before. "Don't worry,

Ramona. Everything will be all right. Mother said so, and I remember when you came."

Ramona felt better. A big sister could be a comfort if she wanted to.

"You got born and Mother was fine." Beezus handed Ramona a clean dish towel.

Minutes crawled by. The long Oregon dusk turned into night. The girls turned on the television set to a program about people in a hospital, running, shouting, giving orders. Quickly they turned it off. "I hope Aunt Bea and Uncle Hobart are all right," said Ramona. The girls longed for their loving aunt, who was cheerful in times of trouble and who was always there when the family needed her. Now she was in a truck, riding along the Canadian Highway to Alaska. Ramona thought about bears, mean bears. She wondered if two pairs of white shoes still danced from the bumper of the truck.

The ring of the telephone made Ramona feel as if arrows of electricity had shot through her stomach as Beezus ran to answer.

"Oh." There was disappointment in Beezus's voice. "All right, Daddy. No. No, we don't mind." When the conversation ended, she turned to Ramona, who was wild for news, and said, "Algie is taking his time. Daddy wants to stay with Mom and wanted to be sure we didn't mind staying alone. I said we didn't and he said we were brave girls."

"Oh," said Ramona, who longed for her father's return. "Well, I'm brave, I guess." Even though the evening was unusually warm, she closed all the windows.

"I suppose we should go to bed," said Beezus. "If you want, you can get in bed with me."

"We better leave lights on for Daddy." Ramona turned on the porch light, as well as all the lights in the living room and hall, before she climbed into her sister's bed. "So Daddy won't fall over anything," she explained.

"Good idea," agreed Beezus. Each sister knew the other felt safer with the lights on.

"I hope Algie will hurry," said Ramona.

"So do I," agreed Beezus.

The girls slept lightly until the sound of a key in the door awoke them. "Daddy?" Beezus called out.

"Yes." Mr. Quimby came down the hall to the door of Beezus's room. "Great news. Roberta Day Quimby,

six pounds, four ounces, arrived safe and sound.
Your mother is fine."

Barely awake, Ramona asked, "Who's Roberta?"

"Your new sister," answered her father, "and my
namesake."

"*Sister*." Now Ramona was wide-awake. The family
had referred to the baby as Algie so long she had
assumed that of course she would have a brother.

"Yes, a beautiful little sister," said her father.
"Now, go back to sleep. It's four o'clock in the
morning, and I've got to get up at seven-thirty."

The next morning, Mr. Quimby overslept and ate his breakfast standing up. He was halfway out the door when he called back, "When I get off work, we'll have dinner at the Whopperburger, and then we'll all go see Roberta and your mother."

The day was long and lonely. Even a swimming lesson at the park and a trip to the library did little to make time pass. "I wonder what Roberta looks like?" said Beezus.

"And whose room she will share when she outgrows the bassinette?" worried Ramona.

The one happy moment in the day for the girls was a telephone call from their mother, who reported that Roberta was a beautiful, healthy little sister. She couldn't wait to bring her home, and she was proud of her daughters for being so good about staying alone. This pleased Beezus and Ramona so much they ran the vacuum cleaner and dusted, which made time pass faster until their father, looking exhausted, came home to take them out for hamburgers and a visit to the fifth Quimby.

Ramona could feel her heart pounding as she finally climbed the steps to the hospital. Visitors, some carrying flowers and others looking careworn, walked toward the elevators. Nurses hurried, a doctor was paged over the loudspeaker. Ramona could scarcely bear her own excitement. The rising of the elevator made her stomach feel as if it had stayed behind on the first floor. When the elevator stopped, Mr. Quimby led the way down the hall.

"Excuse me," called a nurse.

Surprised, the family stopped and turned.

"Children under twelve are not allowed to visit the maternity ward," said the nurse. "Little girl, you will have to go down and wait in the lobby."

"Why is that?" asked Mr. Quimby.

"Children under twelve might have contagious diseases," explained the nurse. "We have to protect the babies."

"I'm sorry, Ramona," said Mr. Quimby. "I didn't know. I am afraid you will have to do as the nurse says."

"Does she mean I'm *germy?*" Ramona was humiliated. "I took a shower this morning and washed my hands at the Whopperburger so I would be extra clean."

"Sometimes children are coming down with something and don't know it," explained Mr. Quimby. "Now, be a big girl and go downstairs and wait for us."

Ramona's eyes filled with tears of disappointment, but she found some pleasure in riding in the elevator alone. By the time she reached the lobby, she felt worse. The nurse called her a little girl. Her father called her a big girl. What was she? A germy girl.

Ramona sat gingerly on the edge of a couch. If she leaned back, she might get germs on it, or it might get germs on her. She swallowed hard. Was her throat a little bit sore? She thought maybe it was, way down in back. She put her hand to her forehead the way her mother did when she thought Ramona might have a fever. Her forehead was warm, maybe too warm.

As Ramona waited, she began to itch the way she itched when she had chickenpox. Her head itched, her back itched, her legs itched. Ramona scratched. A woman sat down on the couch, looked at Ramona, got up, and moved to another couch.

Ramona felt worse. She itched more and scratched harder. She swallowed often to see how her sore throat was coming along. She peeked down the neck of her blouse to see if she might have a rash and was surprised that she did not. She sniffed from time to time to see if she had a runny nose.

Now Ramona was angry. It would serve everybody right if she came down with some horrible
disease, right there in their old hospital. That would
show everybody how germfree the place was.
Ramona squirmed and gave that hard-to-reach place
between her shoulder blades a good hard scratch.
Then she scratched her head with both hands.
People stopped to stare.

A man in a white coat, with a stethoscope hanging
out of his pocket, came hurrying through the lobby,
glanced at Ramona, stopped, and took a good look at
her. "How do you feel?" he asked.

"Awful," she admitted. "A nurse said I was too
germy to go see my mother and new sister, but I
think I caught some disease right here."

"I see," said the doctor. "Open your mouth and
say 'ah.' "

Ramona *ahhed* until she gagged.

"Mh-hm," murmured the doctor. He looked so serious Ramona was alarmed. Then he pulled out his stethoscope and listened to her front and back, thumping as he did so. What was he hearing? Was there something wrong with her insides? Why didn't her father come?

The doctor nodded as if his worst suspicions had been confirmed. "Just as I thought," he said, pulling out his prescription pad.

Medicine, ugh. Ramona's twitching stopped. Her nose and throat felt fine. "I feel much better," she assured the doctor as she eyed that prescription pad with distrust.

"An acute case of siblingitis. Not at all unusual around here, but it shouldn't last long." He tore off the prescription he had written, instructed Ramona to give it to her father, and hurried on down the hall.

Ramona could not remember the name of her illness. She tried to read the doctor's scribbly cursive writing, but she could not. She could only read neat cursive, the sort her teacher wrote on the blackboard.

Itching again, she was still staring at the slip of paper when Mr. Quimby and Beezus stepped out of the elevator. "Roberta is so tiny." Beezus was radiant with joy. "And she is perfectly darling. She has a little round nose and—oh, when you see her, you'll love her."

"I'm sick." Ramona tried to sound pitiful. "I've got something awful. A doctor said so."

Beezus paid no attention. "And Roberta has brown hair—"

Mr. Quimby interrupted. "What's this all about, Ramona?"

"A doctor said I had something, some kind of *itis*, and I have to have this right away." She handed her father her prescription and scratched one shoulder. "If I don't, I might get sicker."

Mr. Quimby read the scribbly cursive, and then he did a strange thing. He lifted Ramona and gave her a big hug and a kiss, right there in the lobby. The itching stopped. Ramona felt much better. "You have acute siblingitis," explained her father. "*Itis* means inflammation."

Ramona already knew the meaning of sibling. Since her father had studied to be a teacher, brothers and sisters had become siblings to him.

"He understood you were worried and angry because you weren't allowed to see your new sibling, and prescribed attention," explained Mr. Quimby. "Now let's all go buy ice-cream cones before I fall asleep standing up."

Beezus said Roberta was too darling to be called a dumb word like sibling. Ramona felt silly, but she also felt better.

For the next three nights, Ramona took a book to the hospital and sat in the lobby, not reading, but sulking about the injustice of having to wait to see the strange new Roberta.

On the fourth day, Mr. Quimby took an hour off from the Shop-rite Market, picked up Beezus and Ramona, who were waiting in clean clothes, and drove to the hospital to bring home his wife and new daughter.

Ramona moved closer to Beezus when she saw her mother, holding a pink bundle, emerge from the elevator in a wheelchair pushed by a nurse and followed by Mr. Quimby carrying her bag. "Can't Mother walk?" she whispered.

"Of course she can walk," answered Beezus. "The hospital wants to make sure people get out without falling down and suing for a million dollars."

Mrs. Quimby waved to the girls. Roberta's face was hidden by a corner of a pink blanket, but the nurse had no time for a little girl eager to see a new baby. She pushed the wheelchair through the automatic door to the waiting car.

"*Now* can I see her?" begged Ramona when her mother and Roberta were settled in the front, and the girls had climbed into the backseat.

"Dear Heart, of course you may." Mrs. Quimby then spoke the most beautiful words Ramona had ever heard, "Oh, Ramona, how I've missed you," as she turned back the blanket.

Ramona, leaning over the front seat for her first glimpse of the new baby sister, tried to hold her breath so she wouldn't breathe germs on Roberta, who did not look at all like the picture on the cover of *A Name for Your Baby*. Her face was bright pink, almost red, and her hair, unlike the smooth pale hair of the baby on the cover of the pamphlet,

was dark and wild. Ramona did not know what to say. She did not feel that words like darling or adorable fitted this baby.

"She looks exactly like you looked when you were born," Mrs. Quimby told Ramona.

"She does?" Ramona found this hard to believe. She could not imagine that she had once looked like this red, frowning little creature.

"Well, what do you think of your new sister?" asked Mr. Quimby.

"She's so—so *little*," Ramona answered truthfully.

Roberta opened her blue gray eyes.

"Mother!" cried Ramona. "She's cross-eyed."

Mrs. Quimby laughed. "All babies look cross-eyed sometimes. They outgrow it when they learn to focus." Sure enough, Roberta's eyes straightened out for a moment and then crossed again. She worked her mouth as if she didn't know what to do with it. She made little snuffling noises and lifted one arm as if she didn't know what it was for.

"Why does her nightie have those little pockets at the ends of the sleeves?" asked Ramona. "They cover up her hands."

"They keep her from scratching herself," explained Mrs. Quimby. "She's too little to understand that fingernails scratch."

Ramona sat back and buckled her seat belt. She had once looked like Roberta. Amazing! She had once been that tiny, but she had grown, her hair had calmed down when she remembered to comb it, and she had learned to use her eyes and hands. "You know what I think?" she asked and did not wait for an answer. "I think it is hard work to be a baby." Ramona spoke as if she had discovered something unknown to the rest of the world. With her words came unexpected love and sympathy for the tiny person in her mother's arms.

"I hadn't thought of it that way," said Mrs. Quimby, "but I think you're right."

"Growing up is hard work," said Mr. Quimby as he drove away from the hospital. "Sometimes being grown-up is hard work."

"I know," said Ramona and thought some more. She thought about loose teeth, real sore throats, quarrels, misunderstandings with her teachers, longing for a bicycle her family could not afford, worrying when her parents bickered, how terrible she had felt when she hurt Beezus's feelings without meaning to, and all the long afternoons when Mrs. Kemp looked after her until her mother came from work. She had survived it all. "Isn't it funny?" she remarked as her father steered the car into their driveway.

"Isn't what funny?" asked her mother.

"That I used to be little and funny-looking and cross-eyed like Roberta," said Ramona. "And now look at me. I'm wonderful me!"

"Except when you're blunderful you," said Beezus.

Ramona did not mind when her family, except Roberta, who was too little, laughed. "Yup, wonderful, blunderful me," she said and was happy. She was winning at growing up.

Meet the Author: **Beverly Cleary**

Books and reading have always been very important to Beverly Cleary. When she was a child, she loved to read books about ordinary boys and girls. She said, "I didn't want them to solve mysteries or have adventures that would never happen to anyone I knew. Most of all, I wanted the stories to be funny."

When Beverly Cleary grew up, she became a librarian and an author of many books. She has written over two dozen of the kind of books she had always wanted to read as a child. She found out that many other children wanted to read the books she wrote too. Mrs. Cleary has received many awards for her books about Ramona, Henry Huggins, and her other "wonderful, blunderful" characters.

You might want to read these other books about Ramona, *Ramona the Brave* and *Ramona and Her Mother*.

Responding to Literature

1. Sometimes characters in books seem like other kids you know, or even like yourself. Have you ever felt as Ramona does in the story? Explain your answer.

2. When Ramona returns to school after summer vacation, she will want to tell her friends about the new baby in her family. What do you think Ramona will say about the time when Roberta was born?

3. Ramona manages to get over her "siblingitis," the "I've got a new baby sister" disease. How does Ramona feel about having a new baby sister at the end of the story?

4. When Ramona says she's "wonderful, blunderful me," she means she's special but she does silly things too. What is one way you think Ramona is "wonderful"? How do you think Ramona is "blunderful"?

Some Things

Don't Make Any Sense

at All

My mom says I'm her sugarplum.
My mom says I'm her lamb.
My mom says I'm completely perfect
Just the way I am.
My mom says I'm a super-special wonderful terrific
little guy.
My mom just had another baby.
Why?

Judith Viorst

Finding Out About the Story

Thinking About What a Character Says

In *Ramona Forever,* Beverly Cleary shows you what Ramona thinks and how she feels through what Ramona says. Notice what Ramona says after Beezus tells her about the new baby.

"She has a little round nose and—oh, when you see her, you'll love her."

"I'm sick." Ramona tried to sound pitiful. "I've got something awful. A doctor said so."

From Ramona's words, you learn that Ramona doesn't want to hear about the baby. She wants Beezus to notice her. You know when Ramona is happy too. Beverly Cleary writes words for Ramona to say that show all her feelings.

Writing What a Character Says

If you could meet Ramona, what would you ask her? How would she answer you?

Prewriting Read what Mr. Quimby asks Ramona. Reread page 31 to find Ramona's answer. Write Ramona's words in your own cartoon. (For ideas about writing turn to the Handbook on page 460.)

Writing Draw a cartoon of Ramona and yourself.
Write what each of you might say.

Revising Read your draft to a partner and ask,
"Does this sound like something Ramona would
say?" Revise your draft and make changes so the
words sound as if Ramona said them.

Presenting Choose two classmates to read
Ramona's part and your part. Coach your actors as
the director of a play would do. Tell them if they
should sound happy or angry or funny.

Extending Your Reading

Expressing Yourself

Choose one or more of these activities:

Make a Quimby Family Album Many things happened to the Quimbys when Mrs. Quimby left for the hospital. Draw pictures of the events, starting with what happened first.

Talk About the Book Did you like _Ramona Forever_? Tell what you liked or didn't like about the story. Be sure to tell why you feel as you do. Pretend you are on a TV news show to tell people about _Ramona Forever_.

Invent New Words The doctor in _Ramona Forever_ made up the word "siblingitis." Play a game with a partner in which you and your partner take turns making up new words and guessing what the words mean. Think of words like "homeworkitis." What could it mean?

Give a Poetry Reading Read the poem on page 37 again. Does the boy speaking in the poem sound angry, hurt, or confused? Read the poem to a partner in a way that shows how the boy feels. Then tell if Ramona would agree with him.

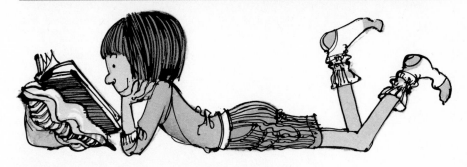

More Books by Beverly Cleary

Ramona the Pest
Ramona really isn't trying to make a great big noisy fuss about everything. Yet somehow she becomes the first kindergarten dropout at Glenwood School.

Ramona Quimby, Age 8
In Ramona's third-grade class, everyone is bringing in hard-boiled eggs for lunch this week. They think the neatest way to crack an egg open is to smash it on their heads. Guess whose mom mixed up the hard-boiled and raw eggs!

Ribsy
Henry Huggins's dog Ribsy, "the best dog in the whole world," is lost. The family who finds him gives him a flowery-smelling bubble bath. Poor Ribsy! Will Henry find him soon, before things get worse?

Ralph S. Mouse
Ralph is in big trouble. The new owners of the Mountain View Inn, Ralph's home, plan to stamp out all mice. At a time like this, a mouse needs a friend. A boy named Ryan may be the friend Ralph needs.

Anna,

Grandpa,

and the

Big Storm

by Carla Stevens

Illustrated by Margot Tomes

Introducing

Anna,

Grandpa,

and the ❄

Big Storm

Grandpa wants to go home to his farm after only three days in New York City. "There's nothing for me to do in the city," he says. Anna wishes her grandfather would like the city better. After all, it *is* where she lives and goes to school. Is there anything that will make Grandpa feel more at home?

New York City in 1888

Anna, Grandpa, and the Big Storm takes place about one hundred years ago in New York City. Carla Stevens, the author, shows you how people lived in the past. In 1888, the electric light bulb and the telephone were new discoveries. Most people did not have them in their homes. In Anna's apartment, oil lamps light the rooms and a coal stove heats the kitchen.

One hundred years ago, there were no automobiles. To get from one part of the city to another, people often rode in trolley cars, which were like buses you might ride in today. They also rode the elevated train, or El, which was pulled by a steam engine on tracks high above the street.

A Blizzard in the City

Carla Stevens shows you what a blizzard sounds and feels like. She writes in a way that helps you hear the wind howl and feel the blowing snow stinging your face. When Anna and Grandpa go out in the blizzard, they find out what an adventure a blizzard in the city can be.

As you're reading the story on your own, discover why Grandpa changes how he feels about the city.

Anna, Grandpa,

and the ❄ Big Storm

Grandpa Comes to Visit

Anna sat at the kitchen table trying to study her spelling words. But it was no use. Grandpa was making a fuss again.

"I want to go home," he said.

"You have been here only three days," Anna's father replied. "I will take you home next Saturday."

"I can't wait that long," said Grandpa.

Mrs. Romano looked at her father sternly. "Now see here, Papa. Next time when we invite you, you can say 'no.' But this time you said 'yes.' And that's why you are here."

Grandpa frowned. "There's nothing for me to do in the city," he said. "Especially on a rainy day."

"Don't you like us, Grandpa?" Tony asked.

Grandpa Jensen looked down at his young grandson. "Of course I do, Tony. I just can't stand being cooped up like a rooster."

Anna pushed her chair back and stood up. How could she get her homework done with Grandpa fussing and stewing all week? She walked to the front parlor and looked out of the window onto Fifteenth Street. Not even the halos of light cast by the gas lamps could brighten this dreary Sunday.

Grandpa came and stood behind her. "Past time for milking. Never thought I'd miss the farm so," he said softly.

For a moment Anna felt sorry for her grandfather. But then he started grumbling again. "How a man can live in a city like this is more than I can understand."

Later, when Anna was in bed, Mama came to kiss her goodnight. "Grandpa fusses a lot," Anna whispered.

"I know," said her mother. "I invited Grandpa to visit us. I thought it would be a change for him after your grandmother died."

"He isn't polite," Anna said.

Anna's mother smiled. "Your grandfather has always said just what he thinks."

Anna sighed. "Still I wished he liked it better here."

"You must try to make him feel at home, Anna. He's an old man."

"Yes, Mama."

"Now go to sleep." Mama kissed her on the forehead. She closed the door quietly behind her.

Anna tried to think what she could do to make Grandpa feel more at home. She and Tony could take him for a walk to Washington Square Park. They could show him the gray squirrel's nest in the big oak tree near the arch, and the daffodils already in bloom around the fountain.

Anna listened to the sleet hitting the skylight above her head. "Oh, I hope tomorrow will be a nice day," she thought just before she fell asleep.

Snow
in the
Morning

When Anna woke up she thought it was still night. No light came through the skylight. She turned on her side in bed and looked through the doorway into the kitchen. Tony was at the table eating his oatmeal. Grandpa was pouring a bucket of coal into the big stove.

Anna jumped out of bed and ran into the kitchen to get dressed. Mama came in from the parlor.

"What time is it, Mama?" Anna asked, warming her hands over the hot stove.

"Almost seven thirty," Mama said. "Go to the front window and see what is happening outside."

Anna looked out of the window. It was snowing so hard, she could scarcely see the houses across the street.

"Don't worry, it won't last," Grandpa said. "After all, it's almost the middle of March."

Mama put a bowl of hot oatmeal on the table for Anna. "Maybe you should stay home from school today," she said.

"I can't, Mama. Today is the last day of the spelling bee. If I win, I'll be in the City Finals."

Mrs. Romano sighed. "If Papa were here, he could take you."

"Where is Papa?" Anna asked.

"He left very early to take his new harnesses to the trolley car station in Harlem."

"What's the matter with me?" Grandpa asked. "Why can't I take her? Besides, I want to stop at Mr. Knudsen's shop and get more tobacco."

"But I want to walk to school by myself, the way I always do," Anna said.

Grandpa gave Anna a sad look. "It's no fun when you're old." He shook his head. "No one thinks you're good for much of anything."

"I don't think that, Grandpa," Anna said quickly.

"But it's snowing hard out, Papa," Anna's mother said.

"Do you think I've never seen snow before?" Grandpa asked. "Anna's going to school, and I'm going to take her. And that's that!"

"All right, all right, go along you two," Mama said. "But take the El, Anna. Then you won't have to walk those eight blocks."

Grandpa put on his overcoat and his hat with ear flaps and his big galoshes.

"And be sure to come right back if school is closed," Anna's mother added.

"We will," Anna said. "Good-bye, Mama. Good-bye, Tony."

"Come on, Anna," Grandpa said cheerfully. "Let's see what your city looks like in the snow!"

Out with Grandpa

As soon as Anna started down the front steps, she knew something was different about this snow. It was not falling down. It was blowing sideways, pricking her face like sharp needles. She pulled her muffler up over her nose.

Anna and Grandpa plodded down the street. The wind whipped the snow in great swirls around them as they crossed Broadway and tramped through Union Square. When they reached the firehouse, Anna saw a fireman shoveling snow away from the stable doors.

"Morning!" Grandpa said brightly. "Quite a storm for this time of year!"

"It caught us by surprise," the fireman replied. "Where are you going on a day like this?"

"To school," Grandpa said. "My granddaughter, Anna, is in the spelling bee finals."

"Good luck to you, little lassie," the fireman said.

Anna pulled her muffler down from her mouth so she could say "thank you." But she felt embarrassed. She didn't like it when Grandpa talked about her to strangers.

They finally reached the corner of Fifteenth Street and Third Avenue. Grandpa turned the door handle of Mr. Knudsen's tobacco shop. But the door wouldn't open.

Anna cleared a spot on the window with her mitten and peered inside. It was dark.

"What kind of shopkeeper is he?" Grandpa grumbled. "He doesn't even come to work!"

"But Grandpa, it's snowing hard now."

"Child, do you think the world stands still every time it snows?" Grandpa looked at her crossly.

It seemed to be growing colder by the minute. The snow, blown by the wind, was beginning to drift along the north side of the street. Only a few people were making their way up Third Avenue.

"Maybe we should go back home, Grandpa," Anna said. "I don't care so much any more about that spelling bee."

"Of course you care, Anna! And I'm going to see that you get to school."

"But Grandpa, the wind is getting so strong I can hardly walk." Anna tried not to sound frightened.

"You don't have to walk. We'll do just what your mother suggested. We'll ride the Elevated."

Anna looked up. It was snowing so hard that she could barely see the train tracks of the Third Avenue El above her.

The
Third Avenue
El

Anna followed Grandpa up the long flight of steps to the Fourteenth Street El station. No one was at the ticket booth so they ducked under the turnstile to the platform. They stood out of the wind at the head of the stairs. Anna could see only one other person waiting for a train on the uptown side.

Anna looked at her rosy-cheeked grandfather. Snow clung to his moustache and eyebrows and froze. They looked like tiny icebergs.

"Here comes the train!" Grandpa shouted.

A steam engine, pulling two green cars, puffed toward them. When the train stopped, Anna and Grandpa hurried across the platform and stepped inside. There were lots of empty seats. They sat down behind a large woman. She took up most of the seat in front of them.

Anna pulled off her hat. Her pom-pom looked like a big white snowball. She shook it, spraying the floor with wet snow. The conductor came up the aisle and stopped at their seat.

Grandpa said, "No one was at the station to sell us a ticket."

"That will be five cents," the conductor said. "Each."

"You mean I have to pay for her, too?" Grandpa's eyes twinkled.

"Grandpa," Anna whispered, tugging at his arm. "I'm almost eight years old."

Grandpa and the conductor laughed. Anna didn't like to be teased. She turned away and tried to look out, but snow covered the windows.

Grandpa leaned forward. "Quite a storm," he said to the woman in the seat in front of them. "Nothing like the Blizzard of '72, though. Why it was so cold, the smoke froze as it came out of the chimney!"

There he goes again, Anna thought. Why does Grandpa always talk to strangers?

A woman holding a basket sat across from them. She leaned over. "In Poland, when I was a little girl, it snowed like this all winter long."

The woman in the seat ahead turned around. "This storm can't last. First day of spring is less than two weeks away."

"That's just what I was telling my daughter this morning!" Grandpa said.

Anna could see that Grandpa was growing more cheerful by the minute.

Suddenly the train stopped.

"What's the trouble?" the woman from Poland asked. "Conductor, why has the train stopped?"

The conductor didn't reply. He opened the car door and stepped out onto the platform. No one inside said a word.

Then Grandpa stood up. "I'll find out what's the matter."

Anna tugged at his coat sleeve. "Oh, please sit down, Grandpa." He didn't seem to understand how scared she felt. How she wished she had stayed home!

The door opened again and the conductor entered the car. He was covered with snow. "We're stuck," he said. "The engine can't move. Too much snow has drifted onto the tracks ahead. We'll have to stay here until help comes."

"Did you hear that, Anna?" Grandpa almost bounced up and down in his seat. "We're stuck! Stuck and stranded on the Third Avenue El! What do you think about that!"

Stranded

hen Anna heard the news, she grew even more frightened. "Mama will be so worried. She doesn't know where we are."

"She knows you are with me," Grandpa said cheerfully. "That's all she needs to know." He leaned forward again. "We might as well get acquainted," he said. "My name is Erik Jensen, and this is my granddaughter, Anna."

The woman in the seat ahead turned around. "Josie Sweeney," she said. "Pleased to meet you."

"How-dee-do," said the woman across the aisle. "I'm Mrs. Esther Polanski. And this is my friend, Miss Ruth Cohen."

Someone tapped Anna on her shoulder. She turned around. Two young men smiled. One man said, "John King and my brother, Bruce."

A young woman with a high fur collar and a big hat sat by herself at the rear of the car. Anna looked in her direction. "My name is Anna Romano," she said shyly. "I'm Addie Beaver," said the young woman. She smiled and wrapped her coat more tightly around her.

It was growing colder and colder inside the car. When the conductor shook the snow off his clothes, it no longer melted into puddles on the floor.

"We'll all freeze to death if we stay here," moaned Mrs. Sweeney.

"Oooooo, my feet are so cold," Addie Beaver said.

Anna looked at her high-button shoes and felt sorry for Addie Beaver. Even though Anna had on her warm boots, her toes began to grow cold, too. She stood in the aisle and stamped her feet up and down.

Suddenly Anna had an idea. "Grandpa!" she said. "I know a game we can play that might help keep us warm."

"Why Anna, what a good idea," Grandpa replied.

"It's called, 'Simon Says'."

"Listen everybody!" Grandpa shouted. "My granddaughter, Anna, knows a game that will help us stay warm."

"How do we play, Anna?" asked Mrs. Polanski. "Tell us."

"Everybody has to stand up," said Anna.

"Come on, everybody," Grandpa said. "We must keep moving if we don't want to freeze to death."

Miss Beaver was the first to stand. Then John and Bruce King stood up. Grandpa bowed first to Mrs. Sweeney, then to Mrs. Polanski and Miss Cohen. "May I help you, ladies?" he asked. They giggled and stood up. Now everybody was looking at Anna.

"All right," she said. "You must do only what Simon tells you to do. If *I* tell you to do something, you mustn't do it."

"I don't understand," Mrs. Sweeney said.

"Maybe we'll catch on if we start playing," Grandpa said.

"All right," Anna said. "I'll begin. Simon says, 'Clap your hands'."

Everybody began to clap hands.

"Simon says, 'Stop'!"

Everybody stopped.

"Good!" Anna said. "Simon says, 'Follow me'!"

Anna marched down the aisle of the car, then around one of the poles, then back again. Everyone followed her.

"Simon says, 'Stop'!"

Everyone stopped.

Anna patted her head and rubbed her stomach at the same time.

"Simon says, 'Pat your head and rub your stomach.' Like this."

Everyone began to laugh at one another.

"Simon says, 'Swing your arms around and around'."

"Ooof! This is hard work!" puffed Mrs. Sweeney.

"Now. Touch your toes!"

Mrs. Sweeney bent down and tried to touch her toes.

"Oh! Oh! You're out, Mrs. Sweeney!" Anna said.

"Why am I out?" she asked indignantly.

Anna giggled. "Because *Simon* didn't say to touch your toes. *I* did!"

FD RAUP

Mrs. Sweeney sat down. "It's just as well," she panted. "I was getting all tired out."

"Is everyone warming up?" Grandpa asked.

"Yes! Yes!" they all shouted.

Snow was sifting like flour through the cracks around the windows. Just then, the door opened. A blast of icy cold air blew into the car. Everyone shivered. It was the conductor coming back in again.

"Get ready to leave," he said. "The firemen are coming!"

Firemen
to the Rescue

Everyone rushed to the door and tried to look out. The snow stung Anna's eyes. The wind almost took her breath away.

The conductor closed the door again quickly. "The wind is so fierce it's going to be hard to get a ladder up this high. We're at least thirty feet above Third Avenue."

Ladder! Thirty feet! Anna shivered.

"Oh, Lord help me," groaned Mrs. Sweeney. "I'll never be able to climb down a ladder." She gave Grandpa a pleading look.

"Oh, yes you will, Mrs. Sweeney," he said. "Once you get the hang of it, it's easy."

"In all that wind?" Mrs. Sweeney said. "Never!"

"Don't worry, Mrs. Sweeney. You won't blow away," said Grandpa.

Anna looked at Grandpa. "I'm scared too," she said.

"And what about me?" asked Mrs. Polanski. "I can't stand heights."

The door opened and a fireman appeared. He shook the snow off his clothes. "We'll take you down one at a time. Who wants to go first?"

No one spoke.

"Anna," said Grandpa. "You're a brave girl. You go first."

"I'm afraid to climb down the ladder, Grandpa."

"Why Anna, I'm surprised at you. Don't you remember how you climbed down from the hayloft last summer? It was easy."

"You can do it, Anna," said Miss Cohen.

"Pretend we're still playing that game. Simon says, 'Go down the ladder'," said Mrs. Sweeney.

"So go now," Miss Cohen said. "We'll see you below."

"I'll be right below you to shield you from the wind. You won't fall," said the fireman.

Anna shook with fear. She didn't want to be first to go down the ladder. But how could she disappoint the others?

Grandpa opened the door. The conductor held her hand. Anna put first one foot, then the other, on the ladder. The fierce wind pulled her and pushed her. Icy snow stuck to her clothes, weighing her down.

The fireman was below her on the ladder. His strong arms were around her, holding her steady. With her left foot, Anna felt for the rung below.

Step by step by step, she cautiously went down the ladder. Thirty steps. Would she never reach bottom? One foot plunged into snow and then the other. Oh, so much snow! It covered her legs and reached almost to her waist.

"Stay close to the engine until the rest are down," the fireman said.

Anna struggled through the deep snow to the fire engine. The horses, whipped by the icy wind and snow, stood still, their heads low. Anna huddled against the side of the engine. The roar of the storm was growing louder.

The Storm
Grows Worse

First came Mrs. Polanski, then Ruth Cohen. Then Bruce and John King. Then Addie Beaver. One at a time, the fireman helped each person down the ladder. Now only Grandpa and Mrs. Sweeney remained to be rescued.

Anna could see two shapes on the ladder, one behind the other. The fireman was bringing down someone else.

"Oh, I hope it's Grandpa," Anna said to Addie Beaver.

Suddenly she gasped. She could hardly believe her eyes. One minute the two shapes were there. The next minute they weren't!

Everyone struggled through the deep snow to find out who had fallen off the ladder.

Anna was first to reach the fireman who was brushing snow off his clothes. "What happened?" she asked.

"Mrs. Sweeney missed a step on the ladder. Down she went, taking me with her," the fireman replied.

Mrs. Sweeney lay sprawled in the snow nearby. Her arms and legs were spread out, as if she were going to make a snow angel.

"Are you all right, Mrs. Sweeney?" Grandpa asked. Anna had not seen Grandpa come down the ladder by himself. Now he stood beside her.

"I'm just fine, Mr. Jensen. I think I'm going to lie right here until the storm is over."

"Oh no you're not!" Grandpa said. He and a fireman each took one of Mrs. Sweeney's arms. They pulled her to her feet.

Anna couldn't help giggling. Now Mrs. Sweeney looked like a giant snow lady!

"Climb onto the engine," said a fireman. "We must get the horses back to the firehouse. The temperature is dropping fast."

"We live only two blocks from here," Mrs. Polanski and Miss Cohen said. "We're going to try to get home."

"We'll see that you get there," John King said. "We live on Lafayette Street." The young men and the two ladies linked arms and trudged off through the snow.

"What about you, Miss Beaver?" Grandpa asked. She looked confused.

"Hey, this is no tea party! Let's go!" said the fireman.

"You come with us then, Miss Beaver," Grandpa said. "You too, Mrs. Sweeney."

Anna's fingers were numb with cold. She could hardly hold onto the railing of the engine. Often she had seen the horses racing down the street to a fire. Now they plodded along very, very slowly through the deep snow.

No one spoke. The wind roared and shrieked. The snow blinded them. One fireman jumped off the engine and tried to lead the horses forward.

Anna huddled against the side of the engine, hiding her face in her arms. It was taking them forever to reach the firehouse.

Just then, the horses turned abruptly to the left. The next moment they were inside the stable, snorting and stamping their hooves.

Several men ran forward to unhitch the engine. Everyone began brushing the icy snow off their clothes.

Suddenly Grandpa became very serious. "The thermometer says five degrees above zero, and the temperature is still dropping. We must get home as fast as possible. Mrs. Sweeney, you and Miss Beaver had better come with us."

"Here, Miss," a fireman said. "Put these boots on. You can return them when the storm is over."

"Oh, thank you," Addie Beaver said.

Anna had forgotten about Addie's high-button shoes.

"Whatever you do, Anna, you are *not* to let go of my hand." Grandpa spoke firmly.

"Mr. Jensen, would you mind if I held your other hand?" asked Mrs. Sweeney.

"Not a bit," said Grandpa. "Anna, you take hold of Miss Beaver's hand. No one is to let go under *any* circumstances. Do you all understand?"

Anna had never heard Grandpa talk like that before. Was he frightened too?

They plunged into the deep snow, moving slowly along the south side of Fifteenth Street. The wind had piled the snow into huge drifts on the north side of the street.

When they reached Broadway, the wind was blowing up the avenue with the force of a hurricane. Telephone and telegraph wires were down. Thousands of them cut through the air like whips. If only they could reach the other side, Anna thought. Then they would be on their very own block.

No one spoke. They clung to one another as they blindly made their way across the avenue. Mrs. Sweeney lost her balance and fell forward in the snow. For a moment Anna thought she was there to stay. But Grandpa tugged at her arm and helped her get to her feet.

They continued on until they reached the other side. Now to find their house. How lucky they were to live on the south side of the block. The snow had reached as high as the first-floor windows of the houses on the north side. At last they came to Number 44. Up the seven steps they climbed. Then through the front door and up more stairs. A moment later, Mr. Romano opened their apartment door. "Papa, you're home," Anna cried, and fell into her father's arms.

Home at Last!

Several hours later, Anna sat in the kitchen watching a checkers game. Mrs. Sweeney, wearing Grandpa's bathrobe, was playing checkers with Grandpa, while Miss Beaver, in Mama's clothes, chatted with Mama. Outside, the storm whistled and roared. Tomorrow would be time enough to study her spelling, Anna decided. Now she just wanted to enjoy the company.

Suddenly Grandpa pushed his chair back. "You win, Mrs. Sweeney. Where did you learn to play checkers?"

"I belong to a club," Mrs. Sweeney replied. "I'm the champ. We meet every Tuesday. Maybe you will come with me next Tuesday, Mr. Jensen?"

"Why, I'd like that," answered Grandpa.

"You can't, Grandpa," Tony said. "You're going home Saturday."

"Who says so?" Grandpa asked.

"You did. Don't you remember?"

"Hush, Tony," Anna said. "Maybe he will stay a little longer. I think Grandpa likes the city better now."

Mrs. Romano smiled. "It took a snowstorm to change his mind."

"You call this a snowstorm?" said Grandpa. He winked at Anna. "When you are an old lady, Anna, as old as I am now, you will be telling your grandchildren all about our adventure in The Great Blizzard of 1888!"

The Great Blizzard of 1888

There really was a great blizzard in 1888. It began to snow early Monday morning, March 12th. Before the snow stopped on Tuesday, four to five feet had fallen in New York City. Seventy inches fell in Boston and in other parts of the East.

The winds blew at seventy-five miles an hour and piled the snow in huge drifts. Everywhere, people were stranded. In New York City, about fifteen thousand people were trapped in elevated trains. Like Anna and Grandpa, they had to be rescued by firemen with ladders.

By Thursday of that same week, the sun was out again. The snow began to melt. Anna went to school and won the spelling bee. And Grandpa walked down to Sullivan Street to play checkers again with Josie Sweeney.

Meet the Author:
Carla Stevens

Carla Stevens says, "Snowstorms are exciting!" Once, when she and her family were kept indoors by a snowstorm, she wondered what the biggest snowstorm might have been like. At the library she read that the Blizzard of 1888 was one of the biggest storms that ever happened. That gave her the idea to write *Anna, Grandpa, and the Big Storm.*

Carla Stevens has written about another true event that happened long ago. About forty years before the Great Blizzard, people were moving west in wagon trains. You may want to read *Trouble for Lucy,* the exciting story of a family's journey west.

Responding to Literature

1. Some people enjoy reading about how people who are stranded in a snowstorm can be saved. What do you find interesting in this story?

2. Pretend you are Anna and are old enough to have grandchildren. What will you tell them about your adventure during the blizzard?

3. At first, Grandpa says, "How a man can live in a city like this is more than I can understand." Why does Grandpa change how he feels about the city?

4. Suppose the blizzard happened on Grandpa's farm instead of in New York City. Name two problems that Grandpa might have in the country.

5. One clue that the story takes place long ago is that there are gas lamps instead of electric lights in the street. Name three other clues in the story that help you know the story takes place in the past.

Winter

Dorothy Aldis

The street cars are
Like frosted cakes—
All covered up
With cold snow flakes.

The horses' hoofs
Scrunch on the street;
Their eyelashes
Are white with sleet.

And everywhere
The people go
With faces TICKLED
By the snow.

Finding Out About the Story

Thinking About the Setting

The setting of a story is where and when it happens. *Anna, Grandpa, and the Big Storm* takes place during the Great Blizzard of 1888 in New York City. In the story, Grandpa says, "Let's see what your city looks like in the snow!" Carla Stevens shows you as she writes:

> "Anna and Grandpa plodded down the street. The wind whipped the snow in great swirls around them as they crossed Broadway and tramped through Union Square."

Ms. Stevens makes you feel as if you are in the snowy street with Anna and Grandpa.

Writing About the Setting

If you were with Anna and Grandpa in the blizzard, what would you tell your friends about it?

Prewriting Try to imagine the city in a blizzard as Carla Stevens described it. Write the city sights from the story in your own list.

City Sights in a Blizzard
1. drifting snow in the street
2.
3.

Writing Write a post card to a friend and tell him or her what you did and saw in the city during the blizzard. Reread the story and use your list to write about the things you saw. Your post card may look like this:

Dear Manolo,
   On Monday morning I went out into a huge snowstorm. I walked through the drifting snow in the street. It was snowing so hard I could hardly see the buildings. It's fun to be in the city in the snow.
           Luis

Manolo Valdez
Grade 3
Lincoln School
New York, N.Y.
         10032

Revising Read your draft to a partner. Ask your partner, "Can you picture what the city looked like during the blizzard?" If you need to, revise your draft and make changes so your post card tells about the city and the storm. Proofread for mistakes. (For ideas about revising, turn to the Handbook.)

Presenting Draw a picture of the city in the storm on the back of your post card. "Send" your post card to someone in your class.

Extending Your Reading

Expressing Yourself
Choose one or more of these activities:

Tell a Story Make up a story about a snowstorm or thunderstorm. Choose a partner to help you tell the story. Start by saying, "It was the worst storm I ever saw." Take turns telling different parts of the story.

Illustrate a City Scene What would Anna have seen if snow had not covered the window of the El? Draw a picture of how the city might have looked from the El high above the street.

Be a Leader Anna taught "Simon Says" to the passengers on the El to keep warm. What game or song could you teach? Pretend you are Anna and your classmates are the passengers. Teach your song or game to your class.

Act It Out Choose an exciting part of *Anna, Grandpa, and the Big Storm* to act out. Decide who will play each character and act out the scene for your classmates. Use words from the story or make up your own.

More Books by Carla Stevens

Stories from a Snowy Meadow
Mole, Shrew, and Mouse love to hear their friend Vole's stories. Vole is a great storyteller. She's smart too. When Mole starts acting strangely, Vole knows just what to do.

Bear's Magic and Other Stories
Every time Bear makes a wish, it seems to come true. In these stories, Rabbit, Bear, and Mouse each want something to be different. What do you think each of them wants?

Hooray for Pig!
The summer is very hot. Even though it's perfect weather for swimming, Pig doesn't want to join his friends. Pig is afraid of the water. What should he do?

Insect Pets: Catching and Caring for Them
Whether you live in the country or in the city, you can have an insect pet. If you can't have a pet dog, a pet cricket may be the next best thing. Find out about catching and caring for fireflies and water striders.

A GRAIN
of WHEAT

A Writer Begins

by Clyde Robert Bulla

Illustrated by Joel Spector

Introducing

A GRAIN
of WHEAT

A Writer Begins

Do you ever think about what you want to be when you grow up? Ever since Clyde Robert Bulla was in first grade, he wanted to be a writer. When he grew up he did exactly what he'd always wanted to do. He became a writer.

Growing Up on a Farm

Clyde Bulla grew up on a farm in Missouri over sixty years ago. He lived with his mother and father, two sisters, a brother, and Carlo, his dog. He didn't have a television or a home video to watch, but there were many things to do and see on the farm. He explored his family's farm, played with friends, and read books. Clyde also did his chores, filling the woodbox and feeding the farm animals.

Life on the farm was fun for Clyde Bulla. There were many places to play, such as the large area next to the barn, the pasture where horses grazed, and the nearby woods. In winter, he skated on a frozen pond and coasted down a hill that was perfect for sledding.

Writing About Growing Up

In *A Grain of Wheat A Writer Begins,* Mr. Bulla writes about what he remembers. You'll know that he is telling a story about himself because he uses the word "I." Because Clyde Robert Bulla is a real person who writes about things that really happened to him, you can find out what he did and thought about as a boy.

As you're reading the selection on your own, find out when Clyde Robert Bulla first knew he had become a writer.

A GRAIN
of WHEAT

A Writer Begins

1

I was born on a farm near King City, Missouri, on January 9, 1914. Besides my mother and father, I had two sisters and a brother. My sisters were Louise and Corrine. My brother was Glenn.

Corrine used to tell me, "The rest of us had good times together when we were growing up. You came along so late you missed all the fun."

I don't think I missed it all. She and my brother pulled me in a cart. That was fun. Neighbors came to our house, and my father played the fiddle while Louise or Corrine played the piano. That was fun, too.

The farmers worked all week and went to town on Saturday night. They went to buy things they needed. At the same time they met their friends. I liked riding to King City in the carriage pulled by our two horses, Mike and Tony. I was five years old before we had a car.

My grandma and grandpa lived in town. We always stopped at their house. I could look out their kitchen door and see the trains come in.

I didn't know until later that King City was a town. I thought it was a great city. On Saturday night the main street was crowded with people. I had my first nickel bag of candy there, and my first ice cream cone. (I bit off the end of the cone, and the ice cream ran down my shirt.) I saw my first movie there, but I can't remember what it was. It was probably a cowboy picture.

There were interesting things to see and do in town, but I was soon ready to go home. It seemed to me that was where I belonged. I liked our house with its little rooms—two upstairs and three down. My father told me it was almost a hundred years old.

In the back yard were trees—peach, cherry, pear, and black walnut. The vegetable garden was there, too. And there were hollyhocks. Hundreds of them came up and bloomed every spring, with bees buzzing among them.

A few steps from the back door was the well where we let down a wooden bucket and drew up water. It was good drinking water, fresh and clear and cold.

Once the well-rope broke. My father had to climb down to bring up the bucket.

While he was down there, I became very thirsty. We drank from a tin dipper that hung in the kitchen. I took the dipper out to the well and waited. My father was a long time coming up. I looked to see what he was doing, and I dropped the dipper. It hit my father on the head.

He was angry when he came up, and he scolded me.

In the front yard were four mulberry trees, an evergreen, and a big box elder. I used to climb the mulberry trees, and I had a swing in the box elder.

Our front porch faced west. I could sit there and see the barn lot with the big barn and small sheds. I could see the pasture and the woods. Beyond the woods I could see Will Sutton's little brown house half a mile away.

My dog Carlo would be with me on the porch. He was a collie. He was the family dog before I was born, but as soon as I was old enough to play outside he became my dog.

Most of our storms came out of the west. I liked to sit on the porch and watch them. The sky would turn dark, almost black. Lightning would split the clouds, and thunder would crash. Wind would blow and bend the trees, and I would see the rain like a gray curtain falling over the woods. It would sweep across the barn lot and onto the porch, onto my dog and me.

Carlo was afraid of storms. He would shiver and push against me. I remember the smell of his wet fur. I would put my arms around him and we would sit there until my mother opened the door and found us.

"You'll be *soaked!*" she would say and drag me into the kitchen. But Carlo would have to stay outside. He was never a housedog.

As I grew older, I played farther and farther from the house. I explored the barn lot, then the pastures, then the woods.

The war came. Everyone talked about the fighting in France. I learned to sing war songs. Someone taught me to march. I marched like a soldier back and forth across the rug with the red roses on it.

My sister Louise made candy and cookies and sent them to a soldier in France. I thought he was lucky, having those good things to eat. She wrote him letters, too. Later he came back and married her and took her away.

2

My mother didn't worry about me as long as Carlo and I were together. She didn't know about the dangerous game we played.

We chased the horses in the pasture. I waved a stick, and Carlo barked at their heels.

One day I ran too close behind them. One of them kicked me.

Corrine found me in the pasture. I was covered with blood, and the mark of a horse's hoof was on my forehead.

For weeks I lay in bed.

Later my mother told me, "It was a terrible time for us all. We didn't think you would live. Even the doctor didn't think so. You didn't know any of us. You talked without knowing what you were saying. Once you said, 'Too much purple.'"

But I began to get well. I sat up in bed. My mother cut out maps and made me a geography book. I kept it for a long time.

I had forgotten how to walk. I had forgotten how to dress myself and tie my shoes. I had to learn those things all over again.

The doctor took my bandage off and said, "There, he's as good as new."

And I was, except for the scar on my forehead. I still have the scar.

That year my family gave me a special Christmas. I had a Christmas tree. I don't remember how it was decorated—probably with tinsel and crepe paper and strings of popcorn. I do remember that it was beautiful.

Just having the tree would have been enough, but on Christmas morning there were presents! There was a drum. There was a box of candles— red, white, and green. There was a little wooden wagon filled with blocks. There were three books— *Mother Goose, Peter Rabbit,* and an ABC book. There was candy, too, and there were popcorn balls and an orange.

Corrine told me Santa Claus had been there in the night.

Just after Christmas there was a snowstorm. The pastures and fields were white, and I was safe and warm inside. I was there with my family. I had my presents. I had my tree.

My mother wanted to take the tree down.

I begged for it to be left up. "One more day," I would say. "Just one more day."

New Year's came and went. My tree was still up.

I had seen a picture of a Christmas tree with candles on it. One day I lighted a candle and tried to set it on my tree.

There was a *whoosh!* like an explosion. The tree burst into flames.

My father picked it up and threw it out into the snow.

I ran into the kitchen. Under the sink was a kind of closet with a small door in it. It was where we kept things we weren't quite ready to throw away—mostly old shoes. I crawled under the sink and shut the door. I lay there in the dark on top of the shoes and I cried. It seems I cried all day.

It wasn't just that my tree was gone. The whole house might have burned.

No one told me to come out from under the sink. No one scolded me when I did come out. My family must have thought I had been punished enough. For weeks afterward there was a burned spot on the ceiling to remind me of the terrible thing I had done.

3

The three Christmas books were read to me until I knew them by heart. From the ABC book I learned the letters—"A is an apple pie, B bit it, C cut it," and all the rest. From *Mother Goose* I learned about verses and rhymes. And *Peter Rabbit* was a good story with good pictures.

I held the books in front of me and pretended to read. I made pencil marks in a tablet and pretended I was writing.

My mother taught me to write *Clyde.*

"Now when you go to school, you'll know how to write your name," she said.

I wanted to read and write, but I didn't want to go to school. Someone had told me tales of what went on at school. They must have frightened me.

Those were the days of country schools. Ours was the Bray School. My sister Louise had taught there before she was married. My sister Corrine had just finished high school and was ready to take Louise's place.

Corrine was teaching for the first time. I was going to school for the first time.

It was a two-mile walk to school. We started off together. Almost always it rained on the first day of school, but this was a sunny September day. I had my new dinner bucket. There was a beef sandwich in it, and a boiled egg and a banana and a piece of cake. But that gave me no joy.

I said, "I know I'll get a whipping."

"I'll be the teacher," Corrine said. "*I'm* not going to whip you."

Later we learned to cut across pastures and through woods to make the way shorter. On this day we took the road. Past Otis King's, past John King's and Mag Elliott's, over the iron bridge and up the clay hill, past George Haynes's, and there was the school lane.

On one side of the lane was a pasture. On the other side was a row of hedge trees. An odd kind of fruit grew on them. Hedgeballs, we called them. They looked like big green oranges and were good for nothing except to throw at fence posts or roll down hills.

At the end of the lane was the schoolyard, with the schoolhouse in the middle. The schoolhouse was white with a red-brick chimney. It had only one room. The blackboard was up front, along with the teacher's desk and the library. The library was a tall green cupboard with a door.

There were rows of seats and desks for the boys and girls. In the back of the room was a big iron stove.

Corrine and I were the first ones there. She wrote *Welcome* on the blackboard. Boys and girls began to come from the farms in the neighborhood. There were nine boys and nine girls. Two or three rode horses to school, but most of them walked.

I was in the first grade with three other boys— Leonard, Lawrence, and Harold. Later Lawrence and Harold moved away, but Leonard and I were in school together for years.

When we were called up for our first class, we sat on a long bench in front of the teacher's desk. The teacher asked a question. What would we buy if we had a hundred dollars? I've forgotten what Lawrence and Harold answered. Leonard said he would buy a horse. That was a good answer for a farm boy. I said I would buy a table.

The older boys and girls had been listening. They all laughed at my answer.

Corrine said, "Why would you buy a *table*?"

I said I didn't know.

On the playground, girls and boys said, "A table—a table! What are you going to do with your table?"

And I knew I must guard against saying stupid things.

Still, I liked school. I was surprised at how much I liked it, although I was sometimes sorry my dog couldn't be there. Every day he started off with me. Every day I had to send him back.

4

It took our whole school to make two baseball teams. Besides baseball, we played ante-over, kick-the-can, dare-base, and Indian. In winter we played fox-and-geese in the snow.

George Haynes's pond was near the school. It was a good place to skate when the ice was smooth and thick enough. Our skates were the kind that clamped onto our shoes. The clamps fastened with a key, and I could never get mine tight enough. My skates kept coming off.

When there was snow, we brought our sleds to school. Each sled had a name. Mine was "The Flying Arrow." Wayne King, who lived across the road from me, had one named "King of the Hills." Coasting down a hill was like flying. Not so much fun was the walk back up, dragging our sleds behind us.

Once during every school-year the boys made what we called a hut. It was a lean-to against the side of the coal-house. We made it of boards, logs—whatever we could find. Tall grass grew under the hedge trees. It dried stringy and tough. We pulled it up until we had a big stack, then we covered the outside of the hut with it. The idea was to cover the hut until it was completely dark inside.

The hut was for boys only. We told the girls they couldn't come in. I can't remember that any of them ever wanted to.

In first grade we had spelling, numbers, reading, and writing. I was slow at numbers, better at spelling. What I really liked were reading and writing. I wanted to learn new words. I wanted to write them and put them together to see what I could make them say.

I would write *apple.* It could be "*an* apple" or "*the* apple." It could be on a tree or in a dish. It could be green, red, or yellow.

Words were wonderful. By writing them and putting them together, I could make them say whatever I wanted them to say. It was a kind of magic.

Reading was a kind of magic, too. In a book I could meet other people and know what they were doing and feeling and thinking. From a book I could learn about life in other places. Or I could learn everyday things like tying a knot or building a birdhouse.

By the time I was ready for the third grade, I had read most of the books in our school library. There weren't many. I wanted more. Except for my three Christmas books, we had no children's books at home. I began reading whatever I could find in the family bookcase.

There was a thick book called *Oliver Twist.* It had words I didn't know, but there were many I *did* know, and I was able to read the story all the way through.

Lee, the soldier who married my sister, went to California. Louise followed him, but for a time she was in Missouri while he was far away by the Pacific Ocean. I wrote this poem about them:

California and Missouri

Hand in hand,
Over the sand,
Down by the sea,
And there sits Lee.
 'Tis California.

Go out and romp
In the swamp
And pick some peas.
There sits Louise.
 'Tis Missouri.

It was my first poem.

I started to write a story, but it was never finished. I called it "How Planets Were Born." This is the way it began: "One night old Mother Moon had a million babies . . . ."

Now I knew why I had said, in the first grade, that I wanted a table. Even then I wanted to be a writer. And didn't writers sit at tables or desks when they wrote?

5

All winter the trees were bare. Winters were so long I was afraid I might forget the leaves—how big they were, what shape, what color. One summer I picked all the different kinds of leaves I could find and pressed them in the big dictionary. When winter came I took them out, so there was no chance of my forgetting.

Leaves were important to me. Trees were important. I must have known every tree on our farm. One of my favorites was the sycamore that grew by the creek. It was the only sycamore in our woods. Its trunk was smooth—pale brown and silver.

One spring day Sam Reed came to our house. He was our neighbor on the north.

"Get an ax! Get some buckets!" he shouted, and he and my father ran off into the woods.

They came back with the buckets full of honey.

"Where did you get it?" asked my mother.

"From a bee-tree," said my father.

A bee-tree was a tree with a hollow in it where bees had made honey.

"Sam found it," my father said. "He saw bees coming out of a hole in the sycamore tree. We cut it down, and—"

"*You cut it down?*" I said.

"We had to, to get the honey," he said.

"You cut down the sycamore tree," I shouted, "just for some old honey!"

I went to the woods. I told myself, It isn't true!

But it was. I could hardly bear to look at the sycamore tree lying on the ground.

For a while I wouldn't speak to my father, and I wouldn't eat any of the honey.

I remember that well. I remember this, too.

I said I wished I knew how to swim. My father went to his workshop and came out with two boards. He had nailed them together in the shape of a T.

"Come on," he said.

"Now?" I asked, because the sky was growing dark, and I could see it was going to rain.

"Now," he said.

I went with him through our woods and into the woods across the road. The creek was wider there, with pools big enough to fish or swim in.

We stopped at one of them. I took off my clothes. He floated the T of wood on the water.

"Lie down on it," he said.

I did, and it held me up.

"Paddle," he said.

I paddled and kicked until I was in the middle of the pool. Then I saw that the wooden T had floated out from under me. I was swimming without it.

"Keep going," said my father.

I kept going, across the pool and back. I could swim!

We walked home. Just as we got into the house, there was a crash of thunder, and rain began to pour. I wondered about my father. How had he known how long it would take to walk to the creek, teach me to swim, and walk back before it started to rain?

There was always work to be done on a farm. Boys and girls had their special chores. My first ones were filling the woodbox and feeding the animals.

The woodpile was in the barn lot. There were big pieces of wood to be burned in the heating stove. Smaller pieces were for the cook-stove.

Sometimes I carried the wood in my arms. Sometimes I hauled it in a little wagon or the two-wheeled cart. I brought it to the back door and piled it in the woodbox in the kitchen.

I took corn to the pigs and chickens. I fed skim milk to the calves.

In summer I hoed weeds out of the vegetable garden and sometimes out of the cornfield.

But there was time to play, time for long walks in the woods. I looked for rocks along the creek. I knew where to find May apples. They grew on plants that looked like little green umbrellas. The apples were yellow and squashy. They smelled better than they tasted. Ripe gooseberries were good. (Not green ones—they were so sour I could never eat one without making a face.) Wild blackberries were even better. Wild raspberries were best of all.

Always my dog was with me in the woods, until one day. He wasn't waiting when I went out in the morning. He wasn't there when I came back.

Days and weeks went by. I looked for him. I called him. Every evening I went out to the front gate and called, "Here, Carlo—here Carlo!" He didn't come home.

School started. I was in the third grade. Wayne King was in the fifth. He came up to me in the schoolyard. "I know what happened to your dog," he said.

"What?" I asked.

"He's dead," said Wayne. He was looking at me, as if he wanted to see how I was taking it.

"He's not dead," I said.

"Yes, he is," said Wayne. "He got poisoned."

I went home. "Wayne says Carlo is dead," I said.

My father and mother looked at each other.

My mother said, "Yes, he is dead. We didn't want to tell you." Dogs had been killing George Haynes's sheep, she said. He had put out poison for the dogs, and Carlo had eaten some of it.

"George was sorry," my mother said. "He knew how much you liked Carlo."

"Carlo didn't run with other dogs," I said. "Carlo didn't kill his sheep."

"George never thought he did," said my mother. "Carlo just happened to be at his place and ate some of the poison."

She was looking at me, a little the way Wayne had. She must have thought I was going to cry.

I didn't cry. But I missed Carlo. Sometimes I still miss him.

7

As I grew older, I began to see that my mother and father were not happy. It was partly because we were poor, but there were other reasons.

My mother had been a town girl. She had gone through high school. That was more education than most people had in those days. She had never wanted to live on a farm. She thought she belonged in town or in a city.

She wanted to do her work in the morning then put on a pretty dress, sit on the porch, and watch the people go by.

Our house was far back off the road, behind a row of hedge trees. She wanted the trees cut so she could see the road.

My father and brother cut the hedge, but it didn't seem to help. Not many people went by.

My father had more education than my mother. He had gone to college to study science and engineering. He wanted to be the first man to fly. In his father's barn he had started to build an airplane.

His father always laughed at him. "Nobody ever made a plane that would fly," he said. "What makes you think *you* can?"

My Grandfather Bulla had two farms. My father went to work on one of them. That was where he took my mother when they were married.

"We won't stay here long," he said. "This is just till I get into something else."

Years later they were still there.

The Wright Brothers were about my father's age. They made an airplane that would fly.

My father was never the same after he heard about it.

It seemed that he and my mother had taken a wrong turn. That turn had led them to the farm. Neither of them wanted to be there, but somehow they couldn't get away. I hoped this would never happen to me.

I wanted to be a writer. I was sure of that.
"I'm going to write books," I said.

My mother said, "Castles in the air."

"What does that mean?" I asked.

"It means you're having daydreams," she said.
"You'll dream of doing a lot of different things, but
you probably won't do any of them. As you get
older, you'll change."

I went from the second grade to the third to the
fourth, and I hadn't changed. I still knew what I
wanted to be.

I thought about writing and talked about it. I
talked too much.

My father told me he was tired of listening to me.

"You can't be a writer," he said. "What do you
know about people? What have you ever done?
You don't have anything to write about."

When I thought over what he had said, it
seemed to me he was right. I stopped writing. But
not for long.

The city nearest us was St. Joseph, Missouri. Our
newspaper came from there. In the paper I read
about a contest for boys and girls—"Write a story
of a grain of wheat in five hundred words or less."

First prize was a hundred dollars. There were five second prizes of twenty dollars each. After that there were one hundred prizes of one dollar each.

I began to write my story. It went something like this: "I am a grain of wheat. I grew in a field where the sun shone and the rain fell."

I didn't tell anyone what I was doing. When my story was finished, I made a neat copy. I mailed it in our mailbox down the road.

9

Time went by. I began to look for the newspaper that would tell who had won the contest. At last it came.

There was a whole page about the contest. I saw I hadn't won the first prize. I hadn't won a second prize either. That was a disappointment. I had thought I might win one of the second prizes.

I read down the long list at the bottom of the page—the names and addresses of the boys and girls who had won the one-dollar prizes. Surely my name would be there. It *had* to be!

I read more and more slowly. Only a few names were left.

And one of them was mine! "Clyde Bulla, King City, Missouri."

"I won!" I shouted.

My mother looked at my name. "That's nice," she said.

Nice? Was that all she could say?

I started to show the paper to my father. There was something in his face that stopped me. I could see he wasn't happy that I had won a prize.

My sister Corrine was there. I could see she wasn't happy either. She was sorry for me because all I had won was a dollar.

Didn't they know it wasn't the dollar that mattered?

I had written a story that was all mine. No one had helped me. I had sent it off by myself. How many other boys and girls had sent their stories? Maybe a thousand or more. But my story had won a prize, and my name was here in the paper. I was a writer. No matter what anyone else might say, I was a writer.

Meet the Author: **Clyde Robert Bulla**

A friend of Clyde Robert Bulla told him that he should write a book about himself. At first, Mr. Bulla said, "I don't know. I've lived a long time. If I told about all of my life, the book might be too long." Later, he decided just to write about the time he remembered better than any other, the time when he was growing up. His memories became the book *A Grain of Wheat A Writer Begins.*

Clyde Robert Bulla wrote more than fifty other books. You may want to read *Last Look* and *My Friend the Monster.* You can find more books by Clyde Robert Bulla on page 135.

Responding to Literature

1. Clyde Robert Bulla calls his book *A Grain of Wheat A Writer Begins*. Do you think this is a good title for the book? Explain your answer.

2. The author wrote about things he remembers doing as a child. What does he remember about going to school for the first time?

3. Mr. Bulla knew that he wanted to be a writer. When did he first know he had *become* a writer?

4. Clyde Bulla probably would have made his mark as a writer even if he hadn't won a prize in the contest. What clues does Mr. Bulla give you in *A Grain of Wheat* that tell you he is the kind of person who doesn't give up?

5. Clyde Bulla wrote about how he became a writer. If you wrote about what you would like to become, what would you choose to write about?

Thinking

Silently
Inside my head
Behind my eyes
A thought begins to grow and be
A part of me.
And then I think
I always knew
The thing I only got to know,
As though it always
Was right there
Inside my head
Behind my eyes
Where I keep things.

Felice Holman

Finding Out About the Story

Thinking About Your Own Story

Clyde Robert Bulla wrote *A Grain of Wheat* to show you what he did, thought, and felt as a boy. He couldn't write about everything that happened to him, so he wrote about things that were important and special to him, such as sitting on his porch with Carlo.

> "Carlo was afraid of storms. He would shiver and push against me. I remember the smell of his wet fur. I would put my arms around him and we would sit there until my mother opened the door and found us."

Clyde Bulla wrote about Carlo because he cared for his dog. He wrote about the special things that mattered to him.

Writing Your Own Story

You can be a writer too. You'll write a story about something you remember learning to do.

Prewriting The list on the next page shows what Clyde Bulla remembered about learning to swim. What else did he remember about what happened? Add two more details to the list. Make a list of your own to show what you remember learning to do.

Clyde Learned to Swim	I Learned to _____
1. Father made a T of wood.	1.
2.	2.
3.	3.

Writing Use your list to help you write a story about yourself. Use ideas from your list to write about something you learned to do and how you felt about learning something new. Use the word "I" as you write. Then add an interesting title to your story.

Revising Read your draft to a partner and ask if he or she can tell how you felt about learning something new. Revise your draft and make changes so your story tells how you felt. Proofread for mistakes and write your final copy.

Presenting Make a cover for your story and write a title on the cover. Put your story in your classroom library for your classmates to read. (For ideas about presenting, turn to the Handbook.)

Extending Your Reading

Expressing Yourself
Choose one or more of these activities:

Start a Collection As a child, Mr. Bulla liked collecting leaves. What is important to you? Collect shells, stamps, or anything that interests you. Find a book that will help you name the items in your collection.

Use Your Imagination Clyde Bulla's sister Corrine asked her class what they might do with one hundred dollars. Clyde said he would buy a table. Discuss with a partner what you would do with a hundred dollars.

Tell About a Book Clyde Bulla thought reading was a kind of magic. What book has worked a kind of magic for you? Is there a book that you remember reading over and over? Share the book with your classmates. Tell why it's a favorite of yours.

Create a Scene Clyde Bulla tells you about feeding animals on the farm and chasing horses with Carlo. Make figures with clay of farm animals named in the story. From paper, make scenery to show the farm.

More Books by Clyde Robert Bulla

The Cardboard Crown
On a strange moonlit night, Adam answers a knock at the door. He opens the door to find a girl wearing a golden crown. Adam believes she really is a princess. Do you think Adam could be right?

Conquista!
Imagine seeing a strange animal for the first time. Would you be frightened, curious, or both? Many years ago in America, Little Wolf sees an animal unlike any animal he has ever seen. He calls it Sun Dog. What do you think it might be?

Flowerpot Gardens
You can grow a garden indoors, since everything you need to know about taking care of plants is in this book. Grow a salad for your family!

Dandelion Hill
Violet is a cow that doesn't want to grow up. She would rather play with the calves on Dandelion Hill than eat grass in the pasture with the other cows. One day, this leads to trouble. Will Violet be forced to grow up?

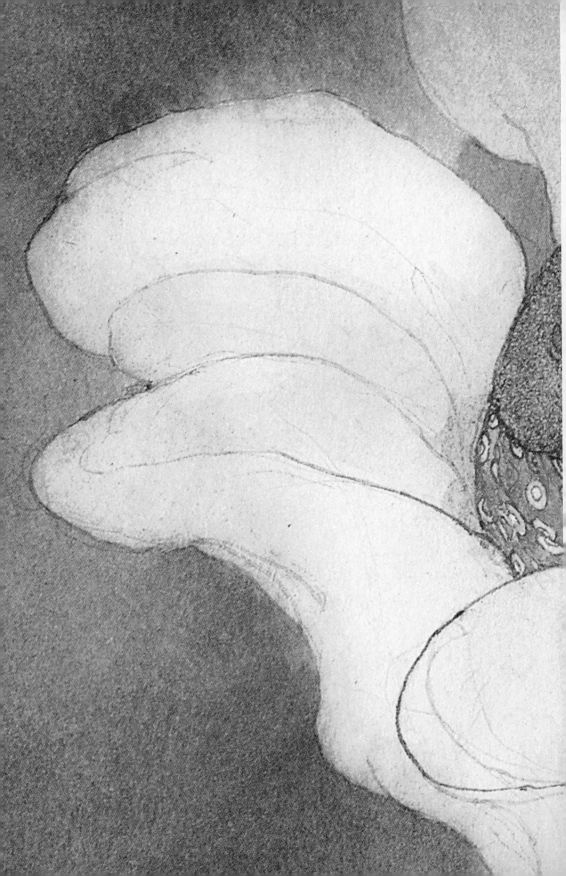

Thumbeline

by Hans Christian Andersen

Illustrated by
Lisbeth Zwerger

Introducing

Imagine what it might be like to be smaller than someone's thumb. How would the world look to you? A puddle of water might seem as large as a lake. A bird would be big enough to ride on. In the fairy tale *Thumbeline,* a girl no bigger than a thumb needs to find a home just right for someone her size.

A Writer of Fairy Tales
Long ago, in the country of Denmark lived Hans Christian Andersen, the storyteller. He was a writer and a teller of wonderful fairy tales. Like all fairy tales, Andersen's story of *Thumbeline* is a fantasy about make-believe people and events.

Characters in Fairy Tales

   To show you that the characters in *Thumbeline* live in a fairy-tale world and not a real one, Andersen gives his characters make-believe qualities. Thumbeline looks like a real girl, yet she's no bigger than a thumb. The animals that Thumbeline meets have fur like real mice and feathers like real birds, but they also talk, wear clothing, and think as people do.

As you're reading the fairy tale on your own, find out where Thumbeline finds a place to belong.

Thumbeline

O nce upon a time there was a woman who longed to have a tiny child of her own, but she had no idea where to get one. So she went to see an old witch, and asked her, "I do so long to have a little child; won't you tell me where I can get one?"

"Oh, we'll soon deal with that," said the witch. "Here, take this barleycorn. It is no ordinary barleycorn, not the kind that grows in the farmer's fields or is given to the chickens to eat! Put it in a flowerpot, and you will see what you will see!"

"Thank you kindly," said the woman, and she gave the witch some money. Then she went home and planted the barleycorn, and it instantly grew into a large and beautiful flower. The flower looked just like a tulip, but its petals were tightly furled as if it were still in bud.

"What a lovely flower!" said the woman, and she kissed its beautiful red and yellow petals. But the moment that she kissed it, the flower burst open with a loud snap. Anyone could see it really was a

tulip, but there was a tiny little girl, very delicate and sweet, sitting in the middle of the flower on its green center. She was no bigger than your thumb, and so she was called Thumbeline.

She was given a prettily lacquered walnut shell for a cradle, and she lay there on blue violet petals, with a rose petal coverlet over her. She slept in her cradle by night, but by day she played on the table. The woman had put a plate on the table, holding a wreath of flowers with their stalks hanging down in the water and a big tulip petal floating on top of it. Thumbeline could ferry herself from one side of the plate to the other on this petal, using two white horsehairs for oars. It was a pretty sight. She could sing, too, in the sweetest, loveliest voice that ever was heard.

One night as she lay in her pretty little bed, an ugly toad came hopping in through the window, which had a broken pane. The toad was big and ugly and wet. She hopped right over to the table where Thumbeline lay asleep under her red rose petal.

"What a nice wife she would make for my son!" said the toad. And she picked up the walnut shell where Thumbeline lay asleep, and hopped away with it, right through the broken pane and out into the garden.

There was a big, broad stream running by. Its banks were all muddy and marshy, and the toad lived here with her son. Oh dear, he was so ugly and nasty, and he looked just like his mother! All he could say when he saw the sweet little girl in her walnut shell was, "Croak! Croak! Croak, croak, croak!"

"Don't speak so loud, or you'll wake her," said the old mother toad. "She could still run away from us, for she's as light as swansdown. We will lay her on one of the big water-lily leaves on the stream. Little and light as she is, it will be like an island to her! Then she won't be able to run away from us while we clear out our best room down in the mud, where the pair of you are to keep house!"

There were a great many water-lilies growing out in the stream, with broad green leaves that looked as if they were floating on top of the water. The leaf that was farthest away was the biggest one too. The old mother toad swam out to this leaf and placed Thumbeline in her walnut shell on it.

The poor little thing woke up very early next morning, and when she saw where she was, she began to weep bitterly, for there was water all around the big green leaf and she could not get to land at all.

The old toad was down in the mud, decking out her best room with reeds and yellow marsh marigold petals to make it pretty for her new daughter-in-law. Then she and her ugly son swam out to the leaf where Thumbeline lay. They were going to fetch her pretty bed and put it in the bridal chamber before she came over herself. The old mother toad curtseyed low in the water to her, and said:

"This is my son, who is to be your husband, and the two of you will live very comfortably together down in the mud!"

"Croak! Croak! Croak, croak, croak!" was all her son could find to say.

So then she picked up the pretty little bed and swam away with it. Thumbeline sat all alone on the green leaf, weeping because she did not want to live with the nasty toad or be married to her ugly son. The little fishes swimming down in the water must have seen the toad and heard what she said, for they put their heads out to see the little girl for themselves. As soon as they set eyes on her, they loved her so much that they would have been very sorry to see her forced to go down and live with the ugly toad! No, that must never be! They clustered together in the water around the green stalk of the leaf on which she was sitting, and nibbled through it with their teeth. Then the leaf floated downstream with Thumbeline far, far away, where the toad could not follow.

Thumbeline floated past a great many places, and the little birds perching in the bushes saw her and sang, "Oh, what a lovely little lady!" The leaf floated on and on with her, and so Thumbeline came to another country.

A pretty little white butterfly kept flying around Thumbeline and at last settled on the leaf, for it had taken a liking to the little girl. Thumbeline was very happy now. The toads could no longer get at her, and they were passing such pretty scenery. The sun shone on the water like glimmering gold, and as the leaf sped along even faster, Thumbeline took her sash and tied one end to the butterfly and the other to the leaf.

At that moment a big June beetle came flying up and saw her. He immediately clasped her slender waist with his claws and flew up into a tree with her.

But the green leaf floated on downstream, taking the butterfly with it, for the butterfly was tied to the leaf and could not get away.

Oh dear, how frightened poor Thumbeline was when the June beetle flew up into the tree with her. She was saddest of all because of the pretty white butterfly she had tied to the leaf; if it could not get free now, it would starve to death! But the June beetle didn't care about that. He settled on the biggest green leaf in the tree with her, gave her nectar from the flowers to eat, and said she was very pretty, even if she was not in the least like a June beetle. Then all the other June beetles who

lived in that tree came visiting. They looked at Thumbeline, and the June beetle girls shrugged their feelers and said, "Why, she has only two legs—what a wretched sight!"

"Oh, she has no feelers!" they said. "And her waist is so slim! She looks just like a human being. How ugly she is!" said all the lady June beetles, and yet Thumbeline was very pretty indeed. Or so the June beetle who had caught her thought; but when all the others said she was ugly he ended up believing them, and did not want her anymore, so now she could go where she liked. They flew down from the tree with her and put her on a daisy. She cried, because she was so ugly that the June beetles didn't want anything to do with her—and yet she was the prettiest thing you ever saw, as fine and bright as the loveliest of rose petals.

All summer long poor Thumbeline lived alone in the great wood. She wove herself a bed of grass blades and slung it under a big burdock leaf, so that the rain could not get at her; she squeezed nectar from the flowers and ate it, and she drank the dew that stood on the leaves every morning. So summer and fall passed by, but then winter came, and the winter was long and cold. All the birds who had sung so beautifully for her flew away.

The trees and the flowers faded, the big burdock leaf under which she had slept curled up and became a yellow, withered stem, and she was terribly cold, for her clothes were worn out. Poor little Thumbeline was so tiny and delicate that she was in danger of freezing to death. It began to snow, and every snowflake that fell on her was like a whole shovelful being thrown on one of us, since we are big folk, and she was only the size of your thumb. So she wrapped herself in a dead leaf, but there was no warmth in it, and she shivered with the cold.

Beyond the wood to which she had come there lay a big wheatfield, but the wheat had been cut long ago, and there was only bare, dry, stubble on the frozen ground. The stubble was like a forest to Thumbeline as she walked through it, trembling dreadfully with cold. At last she came to the fieldmouse's door, a little hole down among the stubble. The fieldmouse was very warm and comfortable living down there, with a whole room full of grain, and a fine kitchen and a larder. Poor Thumbeline stood at her door like a beggar girl, asking for a tiny piece of barleycorn, because she had had nothing at all to eat for two days.

"You poor little thing!" said the fieldmouse, who was a good old creature at heart. "Come into my nice warm room and share my meal!" She took a fancy to Thumbeline, and told her, "You can stay the winter with me if you like, but you must keep my house clean and tell me stories. I'm very fond of stories."

So Thumbeline did as the good old fieldmouse asked, and she was very comfortable indeed.

"We'll soon be having a visitor," said the fieldmouse. "My neighbor usually comes to visit me every day of the week. He is even better off than me, and has a finer house than mine, with great big rooms to live in, and he wears a fine black velvet fur coat. If you could only marry him, you'd be well provided for. But he can't see, so you must tell him the very best stories you know!"

However, Thumbeline did not like this idea. She didn't want to marry the neighbor a bit, for he was a mole.

And so he came visiting in his black velvet coat. The fieldmouse said he was very rich and very clever, and his property was over twenty times bigger than hers. The mole knew all sorts of things, but he could not bear the sun and the pretty flowers, and he never spoke well of them because he had never seen them. Thumbeline had to sing for him, so she sang "Ladybird, ladybird, fly away home," and "The monk in the meadow." The mole fell in love with her for her pretty voice, but he said nothing yet, for he was a very cautious man.

Recently he had dug a long passage through the earth from his house to the fieldmouse's, and he said the fieldmouse and Thumbeline could walk there whenever they liked. He told them not to be afraid of the dead bird lying in the passage. The bird was a whole one, with beak and feathers and all; it could only just have died when winter came, and now it lay buried on the spot where he had dug his own passage.

The mole took a piece of rotten wood in his mouth, for rotten wood shines like fire in the dark, and went ahead to light the way down the long, dark passage for them. When they came to the place where the dead bird lay, the mole put his big nose against the roof and pushed up the earth, making a large hole so that the light could shine in. In the middle of the floor lay a dead swallow, its beautiful wings close to its sides, its legs and head tucked into its feathers. Poor bird, it must surely have died of cold. Thumbeline felt very sorry for it, for she loved all the little birds dearly. They had sung and chirped for her so prettily all summer long. But the mole gave it a kick with his stumpy leg and said, "That's the end of all his twittering! How miserable to be born a bird! Thank heaven none of my own children will be birds—all a bird can do is sing, and then starve to death in the winter."

"You are a sensible man, and you may well say so," agreed the fieldmouse.

"What reward does a bird get for its singing when winter comes? It must starve and freeze, and yet birds are thought so wonderful!"

Thumbeline said nothing, but when the other two had turned their backs on the bird she bent down, parted the feathers over its head and kissed its closed eyes. "Perhaps this was the very bird that sang so beautifully for me in summer," she thought. "How happy the dear, pretty bird made me then!"

The mole stopped up the hole through which daylight shone in and took the ladies home again. That night, however, Thumbeline could not sleep. She made a beautiful big blanket out of hay, carried it down and wrapped it around the pretty bird. She tucked some soft cotton she had found in the field-mouse's house close to the bird's sides, to make him a warm place to lie in the cold earth.

"Goodbye, you lovely little bird!" she said. "Goodbye, and thank you for your beautiful songs in summer, when all the trees were green and the sun shone so warmly!" And she laid her head on the bird's breast; but then she had a shock, for it felt as if something were beating inside. It was the bird's heart! The swallow was not dead, only unconscious, and now that he was warmer, he was coming back to life.

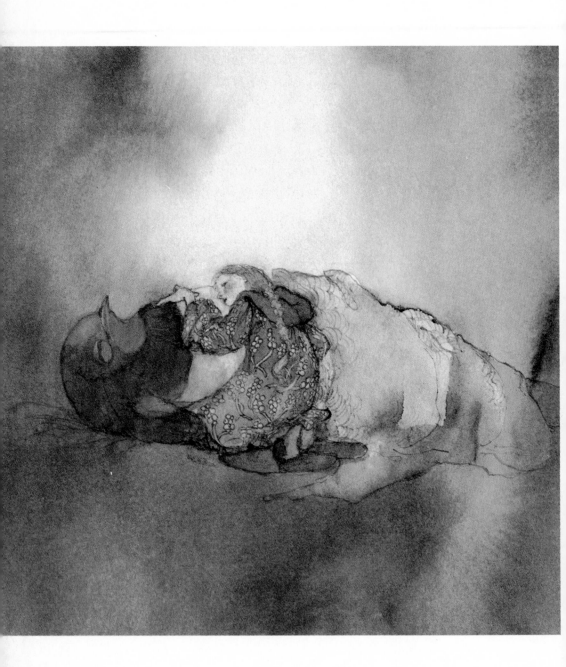

Swallows all fly to the warm countries in autumn, but if one of them lingers too long it freezes, falls to the ground and lies where it has fallen as if dead, and the cold snow covers it up.

Thumbeline was trembling with fright, for as she was only the size of your thumb, the bird looked gigantic to her. But she plucked up her courage, tucked the cotton closer around the poor swallow, and fetched a mint leaf she herself had been using as a coverlet to lay over the bird's head.

Next night she slipped down to see him again. He was awake, but so tired he could only open his eyes for a moment, to see Thumbeline standing there with a piece of rotten wood in her hand, since she had no other lantern.

"Thank you, my dear, sweet child, thank you!" said the sick swallow. "I am so nice and warm now! I'll soon have my strength back, and then I'll be able to fly out into the warm sunshine again!"

"Oh, but it's so cold outside now!" she said. "It is snowing and freezing! You must stay warm in bed, and I'll look after you!"

She brought the swallow water in a flower petal. He drank it, and told her he had hurt a wing on a thorn bush, so that he could not fly as fast as the other swallows when they all went far, far away to the warm countries. At last he had fallen to the ground, and that was all he knew. He had no idea how he had come to be under the ground.

So he stayed down there all winter, and Thumbeline was good to him, and loved him very much. She did not let the mole or the fieldmouse know anything about it, because they would not care about helping the poor sick swallow.

As soon as spring came, and the sun's rays warmed the earth, the swallow said goodbye to Thumbeline. She opened up the hole the mole had made in the roof overhead. The sun shone in on them so beautifully, and the swallow asked if she would like to come with him. He said she could sit on his back, and they would fly far away into the green wood. But Thumbeline knew it would hurt the old fieldmouse's feelings if she left like that.

"No," said Thumbeline, "I can't go."

"Goodbye, goodbye, you sweet, good girl," said the swallow, and he flew out into the sunshine. Thumbeline watched him go, and tears came to her eyes, because she loved the poor swallow so much.

"Tweet! Tweet!" sang the bird, and he flew away into the green wood.

Thumbeline was very sad. She was not allowed to go out into the warm sunlight. The seedcorn sown in the field above the mousehole was growing tall now, and it was like a thick forest to a poor little girl only as big as your thumb.

"You must spend the summer sewing your trousseau!" the fieldmouse told her, for Neighbor Mole, who was so tedious but had a black velvet fur coat, had asked for her hand in marriage. "You will have both wool and linen to wear, and underclothes and household linen, when you are married to the mole."

So Thumbeline had to sit at the distaff and spin, and the fieldmouse hired four spiders to come too, and spin and weave by day and by night. Every evening the mole came visiting, and he always said that when the summer came to an end, and the sun was not as hot as it was now, when it baked the earth as hard as stone—yes, when summer was over, his wedding to Thumbeline would be held. She did not like the thought of it at all, for she could not bear the tedious mole. Every morning at sunrise, and every evening at sunset, she would slip outside the door, and when the wind blew the ears of wheat apart so that she could see the blue sky, she thought how bright and lovely it was out here,

and longed to see her old friend the swallow again. But the swallow did not come back. He had flown far away into the beautiful green wood.

When fall came, Thumbeline had her trousseau ready. "You are to be married in four weeks' time," the fieldmouse told her.

But Thumbeline wept, and said she did not want to marry the tiresome old mole. "Fiddle-de-dee!" said the fieldmouse. "Don't be so stubborn, or I'll bite you with my white teeth! It's a very fine husband you are getting! Why, the Queen herself does not own a black velvet fur coat the like of his. He has stores in his kitchen and his cellar, and you ought to thank Heaven for him!"

So the wedding was to take place. The mole had already come to fetch Thumbeline away to live with him deep down underground. They would never again come out to see the warm sun, for the mole could not stand sunshine. Poor child, she was very unhappy to have to say goodbye to the beautiful sun. While she was living with the fieldmouse she had at least been able to step outside the door and see it.

"Goodbye, bright sun!" she said, stretching her arms up into the air, and she walked a little way beyond the fieldmouse's hole, for the wheat had been reaped now and there was nothing left but dry stubble. "Goodbye, goodbye!" she said, putting her arms around a little red flower that grew there. "Give my love to my dear swallow, if you see him!"

"Tweet! Tweet!" sang a voice overhead at that very

moment. She looked up, and it was the swallow flying by. He was delighted to see Thumbeline. She told him how little she liked the thought of marrying the ugly mole, and going to live underground where the sun never shone. She had to shed tears—she could not help it.

"The cold winter is coming," said the swallow. "I'm flying away to the warm countries. Would you like to come with me? You can sit on my back. Just tie yourself on with your sash, and we'll fly away from the ugly mole and his dark house, far away over the mountains to the warm countries, where the sun shines more beautifully than it does here, and where it is always summer and there are lovely flowers. Do fly away with me, dear little Thumbeline who saved my life when I lay frozen in the dark, underground!"

"Oh yes, I'll come with you!" said Thumbeline, and she sat on the bird's back, with her feet on his outspread wings. Thumbeline tied her sash to one of his strongest feathers. Then the swallow flew high up into the air, over the woods and over the water, over the high mountains where snow lies all the year round.

Thumbeline was freezing in the cold air, but she crept in among the bird's warm feathers, and just put her little head out to see all the wonders down below.

So they came to the warm countries. The sun shone much more brightly there than it does here,

the sky was twice as high, and the most beautiful
green and blue grapes grew all along the ditches
and the hedges. The woods were full of oranges
and lemons, the air was fragrant with myrtle and
mint, and the prettiest of children ran down the
road playing with big, bright butterflies. But still
the swallow flew on, and everything became even
more beautiful.

A shining white marble castle of the olden days
stood beneath splendid green trees, by the side of a
blue lake. Vines clambered around its tall columns,
and there were a great many swallows' nests up at
the top. One of them belonged to the swallow who
was carrying Thumbeline.

"Here is my home," said the swallow. "But if
you'd like to choose one of the magnificent flowers
growing down below for yourself, I'll put you into
it, and you will live there as comfortably as ever
you could wish!"

"Oh, that would be wonderful!" she said, clapping
her little hands.

One big white marble column had fallen to the
ground and was broken into three, but the loveliest big, white flowers grew among its pieces.
The swallow flew down with Thumbeline and put
her on the wide petals of one of these flowers.

How surprised she was to see a little man sitting in the middle of the flower! He was as pale and clear as if he were made of glass, and he wore the dearest little gold crown on his head, and had the loveliest bright wings on his shoulders. He was the spirit of the flower, and he himself was no bigger than Thumbeline. There was a little man or woman like him living in every flower, but he was the king of them all.

"Oh, how handsome he is!" Thumbeline whispered to the swallow. As for the little prince, he was quite frightened of the swallow, for the bird was enormous compared to his own small and delicate self. But when he set eyes on Thumbeline he was delighted, for she was the most beautiful girl he had ever seen. So he took the gold crown off his head, and put it on hers, and asked her name. Then he asked if she would be his wife and become the queen of all the flowers! Well, this was a nicer sort of husband than the toad's son, or the mole with his black velvet fur coat. So she said yes to the handsome prince.

Then a little lady or a little gentleman came out of every flower, all so pretty that it was a joy to see them. They all brought Thumbeline presents, and the best of all was a pair of lovely wings from a big

white fly. The wings were fastened to Thumbeline's back, and now she too could fly from flower to flower. How happy they all were! The swallow sat in his nest, and sang for them with all his might. But he was sad at heart, for he loved Thumbeline, and never wanted to part with her.

"You must not be called Thumbeline anymore," said the Prince of the Flowers. "It's an ugly name, and you are so beautiful. We will call you Maia!"

"Goodbye, goodbye!" said the swallow, for it had come to be the season for him to fly away from the warm countries, far away and back again to Denmark. There he had a little nest above the window where the man who tells fairy tales lives. The swallow sang, "Tweet, tweet!" to the man, and that is how we come to know the whole story.

Meet the Author:

Hans Christian Andersen

Soon after Hans Christian Andersen wrote his first book of fairy tales, he found out that people loved his stories. Kings and queens invited him to their palaces to hear him tell his fairy tales.

The stories Andersen wrote and told long ago are the same stories you can get from your own library now. Some of the tales he wrote are *The Ugly Duckling*, *The Nightingale*, and *The Wild Swans*.

Responding to Literature

1. Many people have a favorite fairy tale. Tell why you think someone might name *Thumbeline* as his or her favorite.

2. The prince might wonder how Thumbeline arrived in the warm country. If you were Thumbeline, which adventures would you enjoy telling to the prince?

3. Thumbeline floats down a stream and flies through the air on her way to finding her home. Where does Thumbeline find a place to belong?

4. You know that *Thumbeline* is a fairy tale and not a true story. Name two things in the story that could never really happen.

The World Is Big
The World Is Small

Group 1: Oh the world is big
And the world is small
So there's lots of room
For the short and the tall.

Group 2: Oh the world is far
And the world is wide
But there are many different ways
To see the other side.

Group 1: You can travel on a boat.

Group 2: You can travel on a plane.

Group 1: You can travel in a dance.

Group 2: You can travel in a game.

Group 1: You can travel on a bus.

Group 2: You can travel on a train.

Group 1: You can travel in a song.

Group 2: You can travel in a name.

Group 1: Oh the world is big
And the world is small
So there's lots of room
For the short and the tall.

Group 2: Oh the world is far
And the world is wide
But there are many different ways
To see the other side.

Ella Jenkins

Finding Out About The Story

Thinking About a Fairy-Tale Character

In *Thumbeline,* Hans Christian Andersen wrote about a character who was make-believe in some ways, but like a real person in other ways. Only make-believe characters can live inside a flower as Thumbeline did. However, Thumbeline also makes friends, just as real people do. Read what happens when her friend, the swallow, offers to take her away.

"'Yes, I will go with you,' Thumbeline said, and she sat on the bird's back, with her feet resting on his outspread wings."

In Andersen's fairy-tale world, a girl can have a friend who's willing to help her. Yet she can be small enough to fly away on his back.

Writing About a Fairy-Tale Character

Think about how Thumbeline is both real and make-believe.

Prewriting Draw two flowers like those on the next page. Add clues from the story that tell you how Thumbeline is make-believe, and how she is real. (For ideas about writing, turn to the Handbook.)

How Thumbeline
is make-believe

How Thumbeline
is real

_____

_____

makes friends

rides on a
swallow

_____

_____

Writing Use the clues from your pictures to help you write a paragraph describing what Thumbeline is like. Tell how she looks and what she does that make her like a make-believe person and also like a real person.

Revising Read your draft aloud to a partner. Ask your partner if he or she can tell that you have written about how Thumbeline is both real and make-believe. Revise your draft. Make changes so that you show that she has real and make-believe qualities. Write your final copy.

Presenting Share your paragraph with your classmates. Listen to their paragraphs and make two lists, one that shows how Thumbeline is real and one that shows how she is make-believe.

Extending Your Reading

Expressing Yourself
Choose one or more of these activities:

Put on a Puppet Play Choose an adventure from the story. Make finger puppets of Thumbeline and other story characters such as the fieldmouse or the prince of the flowers. Ask a partner to help you act out the adventure you chose.

Make a Mobile There are many flying creatures in *Thumbeline,* including the swallow, the butterfly, and even Thumbeline after she is given wings. Make a mobile of flying characters from cardboard with tissue-paper wings. Attach them to a hanger with string.

Tell a Tale Do you have a favorite fairy tale? Pretend you are a storyteller like Hans Christian Andersen and practice telling your favorite tale to a group of classmates.

Be a Fairy-Tale Character Choose a fairy-tale character that you'd like to pretend to be. Act out something that he or she might do. To be Cinderella, you might pretend to sweep the floor. Have your classmates guess who you are.

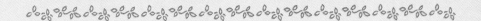

More Books About Getting There

Watch the Stars Come Out by Riki Levinson
It's scary to travel across the ocean from Europe in a huge boat when the only person you know is your younger brother. In this story, a little girl and her brother travel to a place they have never been, New York City.

The Secret River by Marjorie Kinnan Rawlings
Hard times have come to the forest. There are no more fish for father to sell. Calpurnia and her dog Buggyhorse try to help by taking a trip to the secret river. Anything could happen.

The Trek by Ann Jonas
A young girl and her friend think walking to school can be very dangerous. They are sure that gorillas and alligators are right outside their doors. Come along with them, if you dare!

Hey, Al by Arthur Yorinks
For Al, a janitor, and Eddie, his dog, life in the city is boring until a large colorful bird pops his head in the open bathroom window. He offers Al and Eddie a chance to live in a very special place. Would you go?

The Stories Julian Tells

by Ann Cameron

The Stories Julian Tells

Have you done things that you couldn't wait to tell someone about, such as winning a baseball game or getting a good grade on your report card? In *The Stories Julian Tells,* you'll meet a boy named Julian who has many exciting adventures that he wants to tell about.

Julian the Storyteller

Julian likes to tell about himself, his parents, and his little brother Huey. He knows how to tell a good story. Once Julian told a story about what a catalog is. He told Huey that it's a book full of pictures of hundreds of cats that jump out from the pages. Julian also told a story about a strange gift he received for his fourth birthday, a fig tree. This isn't all Julian wants to say. He has more stories to tell.

Stories About Growing Up

You will read three stories that the author, Ann Cameron, has Julian tell. Julian is a character in the stories, but he seems like a real boy. In Julian's stories you will find out how Julian feels about losing a tooth, making a friend, and making a bet with his new friend. Even though the stories tell about different events, they all tell about what happens to Julian and other kids as they grow up.

As you're reading the stories on your own, find out what kind of person Julian is.

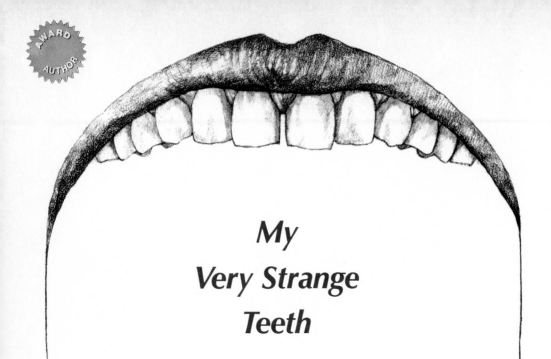

My
Very Strange
Teeth

My mother and Huey were listening. My father
and I were talking.

"Well," my father said, "if you wait long
enough, it will fall out." He was talking about
my tooth, my right bottom front tooth.

"How long do I have to wait?" I asked.
Because I had *two* right bottom front teeth—
one firm little new one pushing in, and one
wiggly old one.

"I can't say," my father said. "Maybe a month,
maybe two months. Maybe less."

"I don't want to wait," I said. "I want *one*
tooth there, and I don't want to wait two
months!"

"All right!" said my father. "I'll take care of it!" He jumped out of his chair and ran out the door to the garage. He was back in a minute, carrying something—a pair of pliers!

"Your tooth is a little loose already," my father said. "So I'll just put the pliers in your mouth for a second, twist, and the tooth will come out. You won't feel a thing!"

"I won't feel a thing?" I looked at the pliers—huge, black-handled pliers with a long pointed tip. I thought I *would* feel a thing. I thought it would hurt.

"Shall I?" said my dad. He raised the pliers toward my mouth.

"NO!" I said. "Not that way! Don't you know any other way to take out a tooth?"

"Well," he answered, "when I was a boy the main way was with a pair of pliers—but there was another way. Just you wait."

He jumped up again and ran to the closet. When he came back, he had a spool of black thread. Thread didn't look as painful as pliers.

"This is a simple way," my father said. "Just let me tie this thread around your old tooth."

"All right," I said.

Very carefully my father tied the end of the thread around my old tooth. That didn't hurt.

"Now," my father said, "stand here by the door."

I stood by the kitchen door, and my father tied the other end of the thread to the doorknob.

"Now what?" I said.

"Now," my father said, "you just close your eyes . . . ."

"What are you going to do?" I asked. I wasn't going to close my eyes when I didn't know what was happening.

"This is a *good* method from the old days," my father said. "You close your eyes. Then—very suddenly—I shove the kitchen door shut. Snap! The thread pulls the tooth right out!"

I looked at the kitchen door. It was a lot bigger than I was—and about twenty million times bigger than my tooth.

"Won't it—hurt?" I was really afraid I might lose my whole head with the tooth.

"Oh, just a little," my father said. "Just for a *second*."

"No thanks," I said. "Please take this thread off my tooth!"

"All right then." My father shrugged his shoulders and took the string off my tooth.

"Don't you know *any other* way?"

"There is one other way," my father said. "Go into the bathroom, stand over the sink, and just keep pushing the tooth with your finger till it comes out."

"Will that hurt?"

"You can stop pushing when it hurts," my father said. "Of course it takes longer—I would be very glad to do it with either the pliers or the doorknob."

"No thanks," I said. I started pushing on my tooth with my finger. "Why can't I push it out here?" I asked. "Why do I have to do it over the sink?"

"When you get the tooth out," my father said, "it'll bleed. That's why you take the tooth out over the sink—so you have cold water to rinse your mouth and stop the bleeding."

"*How much* bleeding?"

"Some. Enough so you should use the sink."

I decided right then that my old tooth could stay in my mouth right beside the new one as long as it wanted—two months, two years, any time.

"I've changed my mind," I said. "That tooth can stay, even if it is stupid to have two teeth where one should be."

"It's not stupid," my mother said, "just unusual. You have very special teeth. I bet prehistoric cavemen would have liked to have your teeth."

"Why?"

"They ate a lot of raw meat," my mother said. "It must have been hard for a cave boy to eat raw meat with teeth missing. But you have two teeth in the space of one. You could have eaten mastodon meat or saber-toothed tiger meat, or anything the hunters brought home."

A cave boy with two teeth in place of one. I wished I had a time machine to go back to the *very* old days—before pliers and before doorknobs—back to the caves. I curled my lower lip under.

"You look like a cave boy," my mother said.

"You should show the kids at school your teeth," Huey said.

"Maybe I will," I said.

I went to my room and made a sign for myself. It read—

See Cave-Boy Teeth
one cent
1¢   1¢

I wore the sign at recess the next day.

My friends came around. "What does *that* mean?" they asked.

"Uh. Uh." I grunted and held up a penny. I couldn't explain. If I talked, they'd see my teeth for free.

After a while one girl gave me a penny, and I showed her my special cave-boy teeth. Some of the other kids had missing teeth, but nobody had two teeth in one space like mine.

I ran all the way home after school to tell my mother what happened. I said, "Tomorrow I'll show more kids!"

I picked up an apple that lay on the kitchen table and took a big bite.

"Ow!" I said, because I could feel my old tooth twist in my mouth. In a minute, without too much blood, it was lying on my hand. "OW!" I said again, not because it hurt, but because right then was the end of my special, mastodon-eating, double-biting, cave-boy teeth.

Responding to Literature

1. Everyone loses a tooth as they grow up. What happened to you when you lost a tooth? Was it similar to what happened to Julian? Explain your answer.

2. Julian's father tries to help Julian solve his tooth problem. What steps do Julian and his father take to remove Julian's loose tooth?

3. Pulling out a loose tooth does not sound like fun to Julian, so he thinks of a clever idea for making use of his loose tooth. What does Julian's idea tell you about him?

4. There are good and bad parts in growing up. What might Julian say is the good part about losing teeth? What would he say is the bad part?

Gloria Who Might Be
My Best Friend

If you have a girl for a friend, people find out and tease you. That's why I didn't want a girl for a friend—not until this summer, when I met Gloria.

It happened one afternoon when I was walking down the street by myself. My mother was visiting a friend of hers, and Huey was visiting a friend of his. Huey's friend is five and so I think he is too young to play with. And there aren't any kids just my age. I was walking down the street feeling lonely.

A block from our house I saw a moving van in front of a brown house, and men were carrying in chairs and tables and bookcases and boxes full of I don't know what. I watched for a while, and suddenly I heard a voice right behind me.

"Who are you?"

I turned around and there was a girl in a yellow dress. She looked the same age as me. She had curly hair that was braided into two pigtails with red ribbons at the ends.

"I'm Julian," I said. "Who are you?"

"I'm Gloria," she said. "I come from Newport. Do you know where Newport is?"

I wasn't sure, but I didn't tell Gloria. "It's a town on the ocean," I said.

"Right," Gloria said. "Can you turn a cartwheel?"

She turned sideways herself and did two cartwheels on the grass.

I had never tried a cartwheel before, but I tried to copy Gloria. My hands went down in the grass, my feet went up in the air, and—I fell over.

I looked at Gloria to see if she was laughing at me. If she was laughing at me, I was going to go home and forget about her.

But she just looked at me very seriously and said, "It takes practice," and then I liked her.

"I know where there's a bird's nest in your yard," I said.

"Really?" Gloria said. "There weren't any trees in the yard, or any birds, where I lived before."

I showed her where a robin lives and has eggs. Gloria stood up on a branch and looked in. The eggs were small and pale blue. The mother robin squawked at us, and she and the father robin flew around our heads.

"They want us to go away," Gloria said. She got down from the branch, and we went around to the front of the house and watched the moving men carry two rugs and a mirror inside.

"Would you like to come over to my house?" I said.

"All right," Gloria said, "if it is all right with my mother." She ran in the house and asked.

It was all right, so Gloria and I went to my house, and I showed her my room and my games and my rock collection, and then I made grape juice and we sat at the kitchen table and drank it.

"You have a purple mustache on your mouth," Gloria said.

"You have a purple mustache on your mouth, too," I said.

Gloria giggled, and we licked off the mustaches with our tongues.

"I wish you'd live here a long time," I told Gloria.

Gloria said, "I wish I would too."

"I know the best way to make wishes," Gloria said.

"What's that?" I asked.

"First you make a kite. Do you know how to make one?"

"Yes," I said, "I know how." I know how to make good kites because my father taught me. We make them out of two crossed sticks and folded newspaper.

"All right," Gloria said, "that's the first part of making wishes that come true. So let's make a kite."

We went out into the garage and spread out sticks and newspaper and made a kite. I fastened on the kite string and went to the closet and got rags for the tail.

"Do you have some paper and two pencils?" Gloria asked. "Because now we make the wishes."

I didn't know what she was planning, but I went in the house and got pencils and paper.

"All right," Gloria said. "Every wish you want to have come true you write on a long thin piece of paper. You don't tell me your wishes, and I don't tell

191

you mine. If you tell, your wishes don't come true. Also, if you look at the other person's wishes, your wishes don't come true."

Gloria sat down on the garage floor again and started writing her wishes. I wanted to see what they were—but I went to the other side of the garage and wrote my own wishes instead. I wrote:

1. I wish I could see the catalog cats.
2. I wish the fig tree would be the tallest in town.
3. I wish I'd be a great soccer player.
4. I wish I could ride in an airplane.
5. I wish Gloria would stay here and be my best friend.

I folded my five wishes in my fist and went over to Gloria.

"How many wishes did you make?" Gloria asked.

"Five," I said. "How many did you make?"

"Two," Gloria said.

I wondered what they were.

"Now we put the wishes on the tail of the kite," Gloria said. "Every time we tie one piece of rag on the tail, we fasten a wish in the knot. You can put yours in first."

I fastened mine in, and then Gloria fastened in hers, and we carried the kite into the yard.

"You hold the tail," I told Gloria, "and I'll pull."

We ran through the back yard with the kite, passed the garden and the fig tree, and went into the open field beyond our yard.

The kite started to rise. The tail jerked heavily like a long white snake. In a minute the kite passed the roof of my house and was climbing toward the sun.

We stood in the open field, looking up at it. I was wishing I would get my wishes.

"I know it's going to work!" Gloria said.

"How do you know?"

"When we take the kite down," Gloria told me, "there shouldn't be one wish in the tail. When the wind takes all your wishes, that's when you know it's going to work."

The kite stayed up for a long time. We both held the string. The kite looked like a tiny black spot in the sun, and my neck got stiff from looking at it.

"Shall we pull it in?" I asked.

"All right," Gloria said.

We drew the string in more and more until, like a tired bird, the kite fell at our feet.

We looked at the tail. All our wishes were gone. Probably they were still flying higher and higher in the wind.

Maybe I would see the catalog cats and get to be a good soccer player and have a ride in an airplane and the tallest fig tree in town. And Gloria would be my best friend.

"Gloria," I said, "did you wish we would be friends?"

"You're not supposed to ask me that!" Gloria said.

"I'm sorry," I answered. But inside I was smiling. I guessed one thing Gloria wished for. I was pretty sure we would be friends.

Responding to Literature

1. Julian says kids tease you if you have a girl for a friend. Why do you suppose some kids would tease a boy who has a girl for a friend?

2. Julian's mother and father might have asked Julian how he met and became friends with Gloria. What would Julian tell them?

3. How do you know that Julian is someone who gives people a chance before he decides if they are friends or not?

4. Some people keep friends for many years and stay in touch with them as they grow up. Do you think Julian and Gloria will always be good friends? Tell why you think as you do.

The Bet

Gloria and I were in the park. I was in one of those moods when I want to beat someone at something. And Gloria was the only one around.

"Bet I can jump farther than you," I said.

"Bet you can't," Gloria said.

We made a starting line on the ground and did broad jumps.

"I win!" I said.

"But not by much," Gloria said. "Anyway, I jumped higher."

"I doubt it," I said.

"I bet you can't jump this railing." The railing went around the driveway in the park.

"I'll bet," Gloria said.

We both jumped the railing, but Gloria nicked it with her shoe.

"You touched it!" I said. "I win."

"You win too much," Gloria said.

She sat down on the grass and thought.

I sat down too. I wondered what was on her mind.

"Well," Gloria said, "I guess you can win at *ordinary* things. But *I* can do something special."

"Like what?" I said.

"Bet you I can move the sun," she said.

"Bet you can't!" I said.

"Bet I can," Gloria said. "And if I win, you have to pay my way to a movie."

"If you lose," I said, "you pay my way. And you're going to lose, because nobody can move the sun."

"Maybe *you* can't," Gloria said. "*I* can."

"Impossible!" I said.

"Well—suppose. Suppose I make you see the sunset in your bedroom window? If I can do that, do you agree that I win?"

"Yes," I said. "But it's impossible. I have an east window; I see the sun rise. But the sun sets in the west, on the other side of the house. There's no way the sunset can get to my window."

"Ummm," Gloria said.

"What are you thinking about?" I asked. "Thinking how you're going to lose?"

"Not at all," Gloria said. "I'm thinking about what movie I want to see."

"When are you going to make your miracle?" I
asked.

Gloria looked at the sky. There were hardly any
clouds.

"Today will be just fine," she said. "Here's what you
have to do . . . ."

It was seven o'clock at night. I was in my room. I had done what Gloria asked. I had pulled the telephone into my bedroom on its long cord.

It was halfway dark in my bedroom. No way the sun was coming back.

The phone rang. I picked it up.

"Hello, Gloria," I said. "The phone isn't the sun."

"Look out your window," Gloria said.

"I don't see anything unusual," I said.

"O.K.," Gloria said. "Now watch your wall, the one across from the window."

I watched. A big circle of yellow light was moving across the wall. It floated higher. Then it zigzagged across the ceiling. Then it floated back down the wall again. It looked just like the sun does coming in the window in the morning. Except the morning sun doesn't dance on the ceiling.

I spoke into the phone. I had to admit—"It looks like the sun!"

Gloria's voice sounded far away. "It *is* the sun. Now look out your window again," she said. "Look at my house."

From the second floor of our house we can see over lots of garages and back yards to the top floor of Gloria's house.

"See my house?" Gloria asked.

"Yes."

"See my window?"

"Yes."

"Look hard!" Gloria said.

And then I saw a person leaning out Gloria's window. It was Gloria. And I saw what she had in her hands—a mirror big enough to move the sun.

"Gloria! You're reflecting the sun into my house!" I said. "You're sending signals!"

It was a wonderful invention! I didn't know exactly what it was good for, but it seemed like it must be good for something.

"Of course!" Gloria said. "I've got to stop now."

The sun went away. Her voice went away. I guessed her arms were getting tired from holding that big mirror out the window.

Then I heard her voice on the phone again.

"Did I do it, or didn't I?" she asked.

"Do what?" I answered. I was so excited about the signaling invention I had forgotten about the bet.

"Move the sun!" Gloria said.

"Yes," I said, "you did it. You win."

"Ummm," Gloria said. Her voice was full of satisfaction.

I knew what she was thinking about—what movie she wanted to see.

And I was thinking how I was going to have to do something I never want to do—at least for years and years and years: pay a girl's way to a movie.

Meet the Author:
Ann Cameron

Ann Cameron got the idea to write about a boy named Julian from some stories a friend of hers, whose name is Julian, told her. When the real Julian was growing up, he really did put wishes in the tails of kites he made with his best friend Gloria.

On her made-up character named Julian, the author says, "I keep making up more stories about Julian, and he keeps growing and changing and surprising me. Sometimes when I'm writing about Julian I feel that he really is a real person and I'm just copying down what he says!"

Read more of Ms. Cameron's stories about Julian in *The Stories Julian Tells, More Stories Julian Tells,* and *Julian's Glorious Summer.*

Responding to Literature

1. Julian learns what happens sometimes when you're too sure of yourself. Do you think Julian acts grown up about losing the bet at the end of the story? Tell why you think as you do.

2. Gloria was probably pretty proud of herself for winning and might not have been able to keep from bragging a little. What would she tell her family about the bet she made with Julian and how she won the bet?

3. It takes time to get to know people. After reading Julian's stories, what do you know about the kind of person he is? How do you know?

4. You have read only three of Julian's stories. Julian has other stories to tell. Would you like to read more of them? Tell why or why not.

poem for rodney

people always ask what
am i going to be
when i grow
up and i always
just think
i'd like to grow
up

Nikki Giovanni

Finding Out About the Stories

Thinking About Theme

Ann Cameron writes about Julian's losing a tooth, finding a friend, and making a bet with his new friend. Does anything she has Julian do or say make you think, "That's happened to me too!"? In all three stories, Ms. Cameron writes about growing up. For example, read what Julian says after he changes his mind about girls.

> "That's why I didn't want a girl for a friend—not until this summer, when I met Gloria."

Ann Cameron shows you that Julian is growing up. Growing up means learning about yourself as Julian does and as people do in real life.

Writing About Theme

How do you feel about growing up? Tell your feelings in a poem.

Prewriting Make two sun pictures of your own like those on the next page. In the first one, add other feelings Julian had about his tooth. In the second picture, fill in a different part of growing up and your feelings about it. (For ideas about writing, turn to the Handbook.)

Julian
losing a tooth

Me

afraid

Writing Reread the poem on page 205. Some poems don't have capital letters and periods, as you can see. Think about what the person who wrote the poem was feeling about growing up. Then use some words you wrote on your sun picture. Write a poem about how it feels to grow up.

Revising Read your draft to a partner. Ask, "Can you tell how I feel?" Revise your draft if you need to make changes so the words tell just how you feel. Write your final copy.

Presenting Poets sometimes read their own poems for others in a way that shows how they feel. Read your poem to someone special.

Extending Your Reading

Expressing Yourself
Choose one or more of these activities:

Give a "Tooth Talk" Think of a good idea for a talk about teeth. You could tell about interesting animal teeth such as those of a saber-toothed tiger, an elephant, or a shark. Go to the library to read and find out about your subject. Tell the class about it.

Fly a Wishing Kite With a partner, make a large kite from paper. Attach a long paper tail. Next, make a list of eight wishes, four for you and four for your partner. Fly your wishing kite.

Make a Signal Code Gloria taught Julian how to use a mirror to send sun signals. Written codes can send signals too. Make up a code that you can use to send messages. Explain your code to others and send messages using the code.

Learn About the Sun Get a book from your library to find out why the sun seems to rise and set. Make a picture that shows how the planets move around the sun. Hang it in your classroom.

More Books About Growing Up

Secrets of a Small Brother by Richard J. Margolis
If you have an older brother, you'll enjoy this
book of poems. Or, if you've ever wondered
what it's like to have an older brother, you'll find
out by reading this book.

Crow Boy by Taro Yashima
The kids at school make fun of a boy they call
Chibi. It's because he is so small. At the school
talent show he shows his classmates what he
can do. What do you suppose his talent is?

Why I Cough, Sneeze, Shiver, Hiccup, & Yawn
by Melvin Berger
Growing up means learning more about yourself.
Find out why your body does these strange
things that maybe you don't even think about.

The Relatives Came by Cynthia Rylant
Have you ever been happy to see relatives that
haven't visited in a long time? That's how the
family in this story feels. The family's relatives
have traveled a long way to visit. Join in their big
family party.

The Rooster Who Understood Japanese

by Yoshiko Uchida

Illustrated by Kinuko Craft

Introducing

The Rooster Who Understood Japanese

Sometimes living close to other people in a town or city can cause problems. If someone's dog barks all day, the neighbors may be bothered. If someone's cat meows all night, the neighbors may not be able to sleep. Keeping pets in the city can cause trouble, as a woman named Mrs. Kitamura finds out.

Mrs. K. and the Ways of Japan

Mrs. Kitamura, or Mrs. K., as her friend Miyo calls her, moved from Japan to America. Even though she lives in a new country, she likes to keep the ways of Japan. Sometimes she eats a Japanese food made from rice, fish, and seaweed called *osushi*. On special days, Mrs. Kitamura enjoys the tea ceremony, which is a special way of making and serving tea. Mrs. K. likes to speak to her pets and

plants in Japanese. She says words such as *dozo,* which means *please* in English, and *banzai,* which is a Japanese way of saying *hooray!*

What Happens in the Story

Yoshiko Uchida, the author of *The Rooster Who Understood Japanese,* chose to write a story about a girl named Miyo who wants to help her friend, Mrs. Kitamura. The events that happen because of Miyo's attempts to help her friend make up the action in the story.

As you're reading the story on your own, find out what Miyo does to help Mrs. Kitamura solve her problem.

The Rooster Who Understood Japanese

"Mrs. K.!" Miyo called. "I'm here!"

Every afternoon when Miyo came home from school, where she was in the third grade, she went to the home of her neighbor, Mrs. Kitamura, whom she called "Mrs. K."

This was because Miyo's mother was a doctor at University Hospital and didn't get home until supper time. Sometimes, she didn't get home even then, and if she didn't, Miyo just stayed on at Mrs. K.'s.

It was a fine arrangement all around because Mrs. Kitamura was a widow, and she enjoyed Miyo's company.

Not that she was lonely. She had a basset hound named Jefferson, a ten-year-old parrot named Hamilton, a coal black cat named Leonardo, and a pet rooster named Mr. Lincoln. She talked to all of them in Japanese. She also talked to the onions and potatoes she'd planted in her front yard instead of a lawn, coaxing them each day to grow plump and delicious.

About the time Miyo came home from school, Mrs. K. was usually outside talking to her potatoes and onions, but today Mrs. K. was nowhere to be seen. She wasn't out front, and she wasn't in back talking to any of her animals either.

Her dog, Jefferson, stretched sleepily and came to greet Miyo as she opened the gate to the backyard.

"Hello, Jefferson Kitamura," Miyo said. "Where's Mrs. K.?"

Jefferson wagged his tail and sniffed at Miyo. Then he went back to his special spot at the foot of the willow tree and curled up to get on with his afternoon nap.

Miyo stopped next to see Mr. Lincoln. He was strutting about in his pen making rooster-like sounds and looking very intelligent and dignified. Mrs. K. had told Miyo that he understood every word she said to him whether she spoke in English or Japanese.

"Mrs. Kitamura, *doko?*" Miyo said, asking Mr. Lincoln where she was.

He cocked his head, looked at her with his small bright eyes, and uttered a squawking sound.

Miyo shrugged. Maybe Mr. Lincoln did understand Japanese, but it certainly didn't do her any good if she couldn't understand what he said back to her.

"Never mind," she said. "I'll find her." And she hurried toward the brown shingled house covered with ivy that hung over it like droopy hair. The back door was unlatched, and Miyo walked in.

"Mrs. K., I'm here," she called once more.

Immediately a high shrill voice repeated, "Mrs. K., I'm here." It was Hamilton, the parrot, who lived in a big gold cage in Mrs. Kitamura's kitchen.

"Hello, Hamilton," Miyo said.

"Hello, Hamilton," he answered back.

Miyo sniffed as she walked through the kitchen, hoping she might smell chocolate brownies or freshly baked bread. But today there were no nice welcoming smells at all. There was only silence and the smell of floor wax.

Miyo went through the swinging doors into the dining room and found Mrs. K. sitting at the big oval dining room table. She still wore her floppy gardening hat over the pile of gray hair that had been frizzled by a home permanent, and she was doing something Miyo had never seen her do before. She was making herself a cup of ceremonial Japanese tea, whipping up the special powdered green tea in a beautiful tea bowl with a small bamboo whisk.

Miyo knew exactly what Mrs. K. was doing because she had seen a lady in a silk kimono perform the Japanese tea ceremony at the Buddhist temple just last month.

Somehow Mrs. K. didn't look quite right preparing the tea in her gardening smock and floppy hat, sitting at a table piled high with old newspapers and magazines. Furthermore, she was frowning, and Miyo knew the tea ceremony was supposed to make one feel peaceful and calm.

"*Mah!*" Mrs. K. said, looking startled. "I was so busy with my thoughts, I didn't even hear you come in."

Miyo looked at the pale green froth of tea in the tea bowl, knowing it was strong and bitter. "Is that our afternoon tea?" she asked, trying not to look too disappointed.

"No, no, not yours," Mrs. K. answered quickly. "Just mine. I made it to calm myself." She turned the bowl around carefully and drank it in the proper three and a half sips. "There," she sighed.

"Are you calm now?"

Mrs. K. shook her head. "Not really. Actually, not at all. As a matter of fact, I am most upset."

Mrs. Kitamura stood up and started toward the kitchen, and Leonardo appeared from beneath her chair to follow close behind. Miyo thought that was a strange name for a cat, but Mrs. K. had told her he was a very sensitive, creative cat, and she had named him after Leonardo da Vinci.

In fact, all of Mrs. K.'s pets had very elegant and dignified names which she had chosen after going to a class in American history in order to become an American citizen. She said animals were purer in spirit than most human beings and deserved names that befit their character. "Besides," she had added, "I like to be different."

Mrs. K. certainly was different, all right. She wasn't at all like most of the other elderly ladies who went to the Japanese Buddhist temple.

"It is because I am a free spirit," she had explained to Miyo one day.

Maybe it was because she had lived in America so much longer than the other ladies who had come from Japan. She never did anything she didn't want to do, although she was always careful not to cause anyone any grief.

Miyo wondered now why Mrs. K. was so upset.
Usually she was full of fun, but today she scarcely smiled
at Miyo.

"I've been upset since seven o'clock this morning," she
explained suddenly.

"Why?" Miyo asked, gratefully accepting a glass of milk
and some peanut butter cookies. "Did you get out of the
wrong side of bed?"

That was what her mother sometimes asked when Miyo
was grumpy. But that wasn't Mrs. K.'s trouble at all.

"It's not me," she said. "It's my new neighbor, Mr. Wickett. He told me that if Mr. Lincoln didn't stop waking him up by crowing at six in the morning, he was going to report me to the police for disturbing the peace! Can you imagine anything so unfriendly?"

Miyo certainly couldn't. "He's mean," she said.

"What am I going to do?" Mrs. K. asked, as though Miyo were the wise woman in the Japanese tale who could answer any puzzling question put to her.

"I can't go out and tell Mr. Lincoln he is not to crow anymore. That would be like telling Jefferson not to wag his tail, or telling Leonardo not to groom himself . . . ."

"Or telling Hamilton not to mimic us," Miyo said, getting into the spirit of things.

"Exactly," Mrs. K. agreed. "He is only behaving in his natural rooster-like way. And besides," she added, "any respectable man should be up by six o'clock. You and your mama have never complained."

Miyo didn't say that they were already up at six o'clock anyway. She wondered what she could say to make Mrs. K. feel better, and finally she said, "I'll ask my mother. She'll know what to do."

Miyo's mother usually found a way to solve most problems. She had to because Miyo had no father, and there was no one else in their house to ask. Miyo's father had died long ago and Miyo barely remembered him.

"Don't worry, Mama will think of something," Miyo said as she left Mrs. Kitamura's house.

Mrs. K. nodded. "I hope so," she said dismally. "In the meantime, I must think of something before six o'clock tomorrow morning."

When Miyo got home, Mother was just starting supper. "Hi sweetie," she called. "How was Mrs. K.?"

"She was worried," Miyo answered as she began to set the table. "She's got to make Mr. Lincoln stop crowing."

"Whatever for?"

Miyo quickly told Mother about Mr. Wickett. "He's a mean man," she said, scowling at the thought of him. "Mr. Lincoln doesn't hurt anybody."

But Mother said, "Well, I can see Mr. Wickett's side too. If I could sleep late, I'm not so sure I'd like having a rooster wake me at six o'clock. Besides," she added, "our town is growing, and we're in the city limits now. Maybe Mrs. K. will just have to give Mr. Lincoln away."

Miyo didn't even want to think of such a thing. "But he's not just any old rooster," she objected.

He certainly wasn't. Mrs. K. had raised him since he was a baby chick, thinking that he was going to become a hen and give her an egg for breakfast every day.

"Besides," she added, "he doesn't crow very loud."

Mother nodded sympathetically. "I know," she said. "Well, maybe we can think of something."

But nobody could. Not mother, not Miyo, nor Mrs. K.

That first night Mrs. K. brought Mr. Lincoln inside the house and stuffed him into a big cardboard carton in her bedroom.

"Poor Mr. Lincoln," she said to Miyo the next day. "He nearly smothered, and I hardly got any sleep at all. He crowed in the morning anyway, but I don't think Mr. Wickett heard him because so far the police haven't come. But I jump every time my doorbell rings. What on earth are we going to do?" she asked, wrapping Miyo into the bundle of her troubles.

Miyo wished she had an answer, but all she could say was, "Mama and I are both thinking hard."

Mrs. K. had been so worried she had spent the entire day cooking Japanese food to take her mind off her troubles.

"I made two kinds of *osushi* today," she said to Miyo, showing her an enormous platter of flavored rice rolled in sheets of seaweed. She had also cooked slices of fried beancurd and stuffed them with rice so they looked like fox ears. Mrs. K. had been pouring her worries into the fox ears all morning, but like her potatoes and onions, they couldn't tell her what to do.

Mrs. K. gave Miyo a platter of *osushi* when she left. "Take some home for your supper," she said. "Your mama will be glad not to have to cook tonight."

Miyo felt that neither she nor her mother really deserved the *osushi*, for they hadn't come up with a single good idea to help Mrs. K. But neither had Mr. Kitamura, and he got a small dish of *osushi* too. Mrs. K. had put it in front of his photograph that stood beside the black and gold altar with the small statue of Buddha and the incense and candle.

In fact, ever since he died years ago, Mr. Kitamura always got a small dish of anything good that Mrs. K. made, and Miyo wondered if he came down from the Pure Land in the middle of the night to eat it. Mrs. K. told her, however, that the food was for his spirit, and that it reached him just as her love and thoughts did, in a wonderful way that she couldn't quite explain.

"I do wish we could think of a way to help Mrs. K.,"
Mother said as they ate Mrs. K.'s delicious *osushi* and
drank steaming cups of tea.

But Mother was so tired at the end of a long day
looking after sick babies and children at the hospital that
she just couldn't find any good ideas inside her head. She
did say, however, that keeping Mr. Lincoln inside a
carton in the house was not the answer.

And Mrs. K. certainly found out it wasn't. On the second night she brought him inside, Mr. Lincoln poked his way right out of the carton and walked all over her house. He scratched the floors and pecked at her sofa and got into a fight with Leonardo, the cat. By the time Mrs. K. got to them, there were feathers all over her living room and Leonardo almost had fresh chicken for breakfast.

"I suppose I will have to give Mr. Lincoln away," Mrs. K. murmured sadly. "But I can't give him to just anybody. It has to be someone who will love him and not turn him into fricassee or stew."

Mrs. K. lost three pounds from worrying and said she was becoming a nervous wreck. "If I can't find a new home for Mr. Lincoln, I suppose I will simply have to go to jail," she said, trying to look brave.

Miyo thought and thought until her jaws ached. How in the world could they find just the right person to take Mr. Lincoln? Then, suddenly, she had an idea.

"I know," she said brightly. "I'll put an ad in our class magazine."

Mrs. K. thought about it. "Well," she said slowly, "I suppose it won't do any harm."

What she really meant was that it probably wouldn't do any good either. But Miyo was determined to try. She had to hurry for Mrs. K. had already said several times that she was becoming a nervous wreck, and Miyo certainly didn't want her to stop being the nice, cheerful person she was.

Miyo's class magazine was almost ready to be mimeographed for the month of October. There were several sections, one each for news, feature stories, science, sports, book reviews, poetry, and, finally, a small section for ads. That's where Miyo thought Mr. Lincoln would fit nicely.

She made her ad very special. She wrote, "WANTED: NICE HOME FOR FRIENDLY, INTELLIGENT, DIGNIFIED ROOSTER. P.S. HE UNDERSTANDS JAPANESE." Then she added, "PLEASE HURRY! URGENT!"

Her teacher, Mrs. Fielding, told her it was a fine ad, and suggested that she include her phone number, so Miyo did. She also drew a picture of Mr. Lincoln beneath her ad, trying to make him look dignified and friendly.

The magazine came out on September 30. That very afternoon, a policeman rang the doorbell of Mrs. K.'s shaggy ivy-covered house.

"I've a complaint, Ma'm," he said, "about a rooster?" He seemed to think there might have been some mistake.

Mrs. K. sighed. "Come inside, officer," she said. "I've been expecting you." She supposed now she would just have to go quietly to jail, but first she wanted a cup of tea. "Would you like some tea?" she asked.

Officer McArdle was tired and his feet hurt. "Thank you, Ma'm," he said, and he came inside. He looked all around at Mrs. Kitamura's home, bulging with Japanese things he'd never seen before. There were Japanese dolls dancing inside dusty glass cases. There were scrolls of Japanese paintings hanging on the walls. There was the black and gold Buddhist altar, and spread out all over the dining room table were Japanese books and newspapers. Mrs. K. pushed them aside and put down a tray of tea and cookies.

"*Dozo*," she said, "please have some tea." She took off her apron and smoothed down her frizzy gray hair. Then she told Officer McArdle all about her troubles with Mr. Lincoln.

He looked sympathetic, but he said, "You're breaking a city law by having a rooster in your yard. You really should be fined, you know."

Mrs. K. was astonished. "Even if I am only barely inside the city limits?"

Officer McArdle nodded. "I'm afraid so. I'll give you two more days to get rid of your rooster. Mr. Wickett says you're disturbing the peace."

Then he thanked her for the tea and cookies and he was gone.

Miyo was proud of the ad in her class magazine, but no one seemed at all interested in Mr. Lincoln. Instead, several people told her how much they liked her feature story about Mr. Botts, the school custodian, who was retiring.

She had written, "Say good-bye to the best custodian Hawthorn School ever had. Mr. Botts is retiring because he is getting tired. At the age of sixty-five, who wouldn't? He and Mrs. Botts are going to Far Creek. He is going to eat a lot and sleep a lot and maybe go fishing. So, so long, Mr. Botts. And good luck!"

Her teacher, Mrs. Fielding, told her it was a fine story.

On her way home, Miyo ran into Mr. Botts himself. He told her it was the first time in his entire life that anyone had written a feature story about him.

When he got home that night, he took off his shoes, sat in his favorite chair, and read the magazine from cover to cover. At the bottom of page twenty, he saw Miyo's ad about Mr. Lincoln.

"Tami," he said to Mrs. Botts, who happened to be Japanese, "how would you like to have a rooster?"

"A what?"

"A rooster," Mr. Botts repeated. "One that understands Japanese."

Mrs. Botts thought that Mr. Botts had had too much excitement, what with his retirement party at school and all. But he kept right on talking.

"When we move to Far Creek, didn't you say you were going to grow vegetables and raise chickens while I go hunting and fishing?"

Mrs. Botts remembered having said something like that. "Yes, I guess I did."

"Well, if you're going to raise chickens, you'll need a rooster."

"Why, I guess that's so."

"Then we might as well have one that's friendly and dignified," Mr. Botts said, and he went right to the telephone to call Miyo.

"I'll take that rooster you want to find a home for," he said. "My wife, Tami, could talk to it in Japanese too."

Miyo couldn't believe it. Someone had actually read her ad and that someone was Mr. Botts and his wife. They would give Mr. Lincoln a fine home and surely wouldn't turn him into fricassee or stew. At last, she had done something to help Mrs. K. and keep her from becoming a nervous wreck. As soon as she told Mother, she ran right over to tell Mrs. K. the good news.

Mrs. K. was just about to stuff Mr. Lincoln into a wooden crate for the night. When Miyo told her that Mr. Lincoln would have a nice half-Japanese home in Far Creek with Mr. and Mrs. Botts, Mrs. K. gave Miyo such a hug she almost squeezed the breath out of her.

"Hooray! *Banzai!*" Mrs. K. said happily. "Tomorrow we will have a party to celebrate. I shall invite you and your mama, and Mr. and Mrs. Botts." And because Mrs. K. felt so relieved and happy, she even decided to invite Mr. Wickett.

"Even though you are a cross man," she said to him, "I suppose you were right. A rooster shouldn't live in a small pen at the edge of town. He should live in the country where he'll have some hens to talk to and nobody will care if he crows at the sun."

Mr. Wickett was a little embarrassed to come to Mrs. K.'s party, but he was too lonely to say no. He came with a box of chocolate-dipped cherries and said, "I'm sorry I caused such a commotion."

But Mrs. K. told him he needn't be sorry. "Life needs a little stirring up now and then," she admitted. "Besides," she added, "now both Mr. Lincoln and I have found new friends."

Miyo and her mother brought a caramel cake with Mr. Lincoln's initials on it and Mr. and Mrs. Botts brought Mrs. K. a philodendron plant. "Maybe you can talk to it in Japanese now instead of to Mr. Lincoln," Mrs. Botts said, "and don't worry, I'll take good care of him."

"You come on out to visit us and your rooster any time you like," Mr. Botts added.

Miyo's mother promised that one day soon she would drive them all up to Far Creek to see how Mr. Lincoln liked his new home.

When the party was over, Mr. Botts carried Mr. Lincoln in his crate to his station wagon. Mr. Lincoln gave a polite squawk of farewell and Mrs. K. promised she would come visit him soon.

"Good-bye, Mr. Lincoln. Good-bye, Mr. and Mrs. Botts," Miyo called.

From inside Mrs. K.'s kitchen, Hamilton, the parrot, screeched. "Good-bye, Mr. Lincoln. Good-bye."

Jefferson roused himself from his bed near the stove and came outside to wag his tail at everybody, and Leonardo rubbed up against Mrs. K.'s legs to remind her that he was still there.

Then Mr. Botts honked his horn and they were gone.

"I hope we'll see each other again soon," Mr. Wickett said to Mrs. K.

"Good night, Mr. Wickett," she answered. "I'm sure we will."

Miyo and her mother thanked Mrs. K. for the nice party and went home, leaving her to say good night to her potatoes and onions before going inside.

"Do you think she'll miss Mr. Lincoln a lot?" Miyo asked.

"She will for a while," Mother answered, "but now she has a new friend and neighbor to talk to."

Miyo nodded. That was true. And even if Mr. Wickett couldn't understand Japanese, at least he could answer back, and maybe that was even better than having an intelligent rooster around.

Miyo was glad everything had turned out so well, and went to bed feeling good inside.

"Good night, Mama," she called softly to her mother.

"Good night, Miyo," Mother answered as she tucked her in.

Then, one by one, the lights went out in all the houses along the street, and soon only the sounds of the insects filled the dark night air.

Meet the Author: **Yoshiko Uchida**

Yoshiko Uchida has a friend who is a little like Mrs. K. in *The Rooster Who Understood Japanese*. Ms. Uchida says her friend does things differently from most other people. For example, most people plant flowers around their houses, but Ms. Uchida's friend plants vegetables instead. Yoshiko Uchida decided to write a story about a person who is like her real-life friend.

Yoshiko Uchida has written many other books about other interesting people. You may want to read *Sumi and the Goat and the Tokyo Express* and *Sumi's Special Happening*.

Responding to Literature

1. When Miyo visits Mrs. K. after school, Miyo thinks something is wrong. How does Miyo know her friend is troubled? How can you tell when a friend has a problem?

2. Suppose that Mr. Lincoln could understand Japanese *and* speak English. What would he tell Mr. and Mrs. Botts about how Mrs. Kitamura tried to keep him quiet?

3. Mrs. Kitamura has a tough problem, but she also has a good friend. What does Miyo do to help Mrs. Kitamura solve her problem?

4. Miyo figures out one way to solve the problem of a rooster bothering neighbors in the city. If Mrs. Kitamura chooses to get a new pet, what would be a better choice? Why?

A bright red flower he wears on his head;
His beautiful coat needs no thimble nor thread;
And though he's not fearsome, I'll have you know
Ten thousand doors open when he says so!
What is it?

Chinese rhyme

Finding Out About the Story

Thinking About Goal and Outcome

In *The Rooster Who Understood Japanese,*
Yoshiko Uchida tells you how much Miyo wants to
reach her goal of finding a home for Mr. Lincoln.
Read what Ms. Uchida writes about Miyo.

"Miyo thought and thought until her jaws ached. How in
the world could they find just the right person to take Mr.
Lincoln?"

Ms. Uchida then writes about Miyo's attempt to
reach her goal. Miyo writes an ad to find a home for
Mr. Lincoln. Finally, the author shows how Miyo's ad
leads to the happy outcome of the story. Miyo finds
a good home for Mr. Lincoln.

Writing About Goal and Outcome

Suppose Miyo hadn't put an ad in the paper. What
else could she have done? How else might the story
have ended? Write a new story ending.

Goal: Finding a new
home for Mr. Lincoln

How Miyo reaches
her goal

Another way to
reach her goal

Prewriting Draw boxes such as the ones above. In the first box, write how Miyo reaches her goal in the story. In the second box, write a new way Miyo could have reached her goal.

Writing Be an author. Use your idea to write a new ending for *The Rooster Who Understood Japanese.*

Revising Read your draft aloud to a partner. Ask, "Does my ending tell how Miyo reaches her goal?" Revise your draft and make changes if necessary. Proofread for errors and write your final copy.

Presenting Share your story ending with your class. Listen to your classmates' story endings. Discuss how many different ideas there are. (For ideas about presenting, turn to the Handbook.)

Extending Your Reading

Expressing Yourself
Choose one or more of these activities:

Act It Out Find a part of *The Rooster Who Understood Japanese* that you think would be fun to do as a play. Practice your play with a group of classmates before you perform for your class.

Start a Class Magazine Miyo's class magazine includes news stories, poetry, book reviews, and ads. What would you include in a class magazine? Make up a sample page and present your ideas to your classmates. Work together on the magazine.

Tell How Something Is Used Mrs. K. keeps many objects in her house that remind her of Japan. Bring to school some objects or pictures of objects from another country. Tell your classmates how they are used by people in that country.

More Books About Animals

The Day Jimmy's Boa Ate the Wash
by Trinka Hakes Noble
The class trip to the farm is pretty dull until the pigs get in the schoolbus and the haystack falls on top of the cow. As if that isn't enough, Jimmy's boa constrictor gets loose. Does this sound like a boring trip to you?

A Bird's Body by Joanna Cole
Have you ever wondered how birds are able to fly? Take a close-up look at a parakeet and a cockatiel. This book tells you how a bird's body makes flying possible.

Harry's Dog by Barbara Ann Porte
Harry wants to keep his new dog Girl very much. There's only one problem, but it's a big one. Harry's father sneezes whenever Girl is near. Will Harry be able to keep his dog?

Cross-Country Cat by Mary Calhoun
Henry the cat is accidentally left behind on a snowy mountain near his family's mountain cabin. Luckily, one of the family members made Henry a cat-sized pair of skis. This may be the ideal time for Henry to try them out.

Amigo

by Byrd Baylor

Illustrated by Garth Williams

Amigo

Have you ever seen a wild animal and wished that you could be friends with it? Did you ever spot an animal watching you and wonder what it might be thinking? A boy named Francisco dreams of having a pet that he can call *amigo,* the Spanish word for friend. At the same time, a certain animal dreams of having Francisco for a friend.

Animals of the Southwest Desert

The pet Francisco dreams of is a dog, but he learns that a dog is too expensive to keep. When Francisco's father tells him that he may have a small, wild animal for a pet, Francisco tries to imagine which animal could be his *amigo.*

246

Only certain animals can live in the hot, dry desert where Francisco lives. When he walks in the desert hills or valleys, Francisco may meet lizards, snakes, hawks, or furry animals called prairie dogs. Early each morning, the prairie dogs pop out of their holes to eat breakfast. If an enemy comes near, a watchful prairie dog barks a warning that sends the prairie dog family back underground. As Francisco knows, prairie dogs are careful about whom they let near them.

A Desert Story

Byrd Baylor, the author of *Amigo,* chose to tell her story in a poem. She wrote about two characters, a boy and a wild animal, who live in a desert. By choosing the desert as the setting, Ms. Baylor wrote a story that could not happen anywhere else.

As you're reading this part of the story poem on your own, find out how a boy and a desert animal know they are friends at last.

Amigo

Francisco's mother tries to help him think of a small, wild animal that would make a good pet. However, a lizard, a bird, and a frog just aren't the kinds of pets Francisco wants. When Francisco's mother suggests a prairie dog, he stops to think. Could a prairie dog be the right pet for him?

"A prairie dog would be easy to find.
Of course, I had a *real* dog in my mind
But
If I try
I think that I
Could love
A prairie dog . . .
A tiny black-eyed, run-around
Hole-in-the-ground
Squeak-a-dry-sound
Prairie dog,
A very
Merry
Prairie
Dog."

Francisco's father said,
"You'd have to win his love
Before you tame him."

"Yes, I will win his love.
Then I will name him
Amigo.
That's the name I was saving
For some big hound—
But I think it will do
For a little run-around."

His mother smiled.
"How do you tame a prairie dog,
A thing that's wild?
How do you make him walk beside
A human child?"

"I'll give him presents
Like water and seeds
And tall sweet weeds.
I'll give him love
And whatever he needs."

Francisco hurried
To Prairie-Dog Town.
Very quietly
He sat down
On a rocky slope
To watch and wait
And dream and hope.

Prairie-Dog Town is a town under ground,
All tunnel and burrow and hilly mound . . .
The busiest town for miles around.
Ten little heads popped out of the earth
And looked around curiously
And jabbered furiously
And frowned at Francisco for all they were worth.

He wanted them to know that he
Was a friend, a brother,
Wanted them to see him
Simply as another
Desert creature
Who meant no harm.
So he lay down
With his head on his arm.
The sun was warm.
He nestled deep
Into clumps of grass.
Time passed. And then,
Francisco fell asleep.

When he opened his eyes
There wasn't a sound.
He sat up
And looked around
And found
One prairie dog still sitting in his place.
He seemed to be studying Francisco's face.

"Can that be Amigo?
Does he read my mind?
Does he know he's the one
That I came to find?"

Very gently he whispered
"Amigo . . ."
The word
Was so soft
It could only be heard
By one prairie dog
And one low-flying bird . . .
"Amigo . . ."
It was half laugh, half song,
The kind of word that floats along.

That day wherever Francisco went
He went with his dreams and he went content.
And he went with a hop and he went with a hope
And he jumped over rocks like an antelope.

Now you know Francisco
And the way he planned
To tame him a friend
In that desert land.
But you still don't know—
Though you very soon will—
What creature was hiding
Behind that hill . . .

Look
Toward the mountain,
There
Toward the sun.
See that brown speck
Dart and run?

That is Amigo.

The desert is wide
And the rocks are tall.
You might not notice
A creature so small.
But that is Amigo,
The prairie-dog child
Who runs with the wind
When the wind runs wild.

Just one summer old,
Adventurous and bold,
He's small enough to look
A tortoise in the eye,
Or exchange remarks
With a passing fly,
And brave enough to jump
At stars in the sky—
He never really caught one
But he likes to try.

Yes, this is Amigo . . .
Always full of ideas,
Saying summer is *his*—
And maybe it is—
To run through.

But should he be running
So fast and so far?
Why isn't he home
Where his brothers are,
In the dim burrows
Which wind far down
Below the surface
Of Prairie-Dog Town?

There
Old prairie dogs sit in the sun
Keeping watch through the summer day
While the little ones dodge in and out
Like children at play.

But Amigo isn't there.
He's *everywhere*,
Following every path he knows.
He doesn't worry,
He only *goes* . . .

And where is he going?
What does he seek?
Why does he gaze
At the mountain peak?

Amigo runs to a certain hill.
There he stops and waits until
He hears the sound of a boy's easy laughter.
Then he knows he's found what he came after:
That boy!

Amigo sits,
Quiet as a stone,
And sees the boy
Walking alone
And carrying a heavy pail
Of water down the rocky trail
And singing.
Ah, what a sound!
Amigo found
It going round
His head all day.
It would not go away—
That sound of singing,
Ringing
In his head.

He said,
"I know every sound for miles around,
Every small and quiet sound—
Like earthworms walking underground
And the whisper of quail
And the wet creaking wail
Of baby toads after a rain,
And the rustle of grass
Where a deer has lain.
Yes,
I think there's many a sound
Pleasant enough to have around.

But
Human boys
Make the finest
Kind of noise
I ever heard—
Better than water
Or wind or bird."

This boy was a little thing—
Only so high.
But he seemed to Amigo
To reach the sky,
Tall as a mountain,
Brown and strong.
Amigo followed him
All day long.

He heard his whistle
And he heard his song
Carried by the wind,
Light as a feather.

Amigo said,
"I wonder whether
He ever saw me
Peeping from under
That mesquite tree
And popping up
From clumps of grass
Along the way
To see him pass."

But his mother said,
"Be careful, my child.
A human boy
Is very wild."

Amigo said,
"I'll tame him if it takes a year.
The sound of that boy is all I want to hear!"

"You can't mean that!
Better go play with the
Old pack rat."

The prairie dogs listened
With great surprise.
You could tell what they thought
By the look in their eyes.
One finally said, as he gazed at the sun,
"Better learn from those who are wise, little one.
Mountain is your friend.
Wind is your toy.
Let's stop this talk about
A human boy."

A hundred aunts, uncles and cousins agreed.
"That's right," they said,
  And they wiggled their whiskers
  And nodded their heads.
"Oh, yes, that's right," they said.
"That's right."

But Amigo told them,
"He doesn't look wild.
  I know if I try
  I can tame that child."

"How about an ant?"

"An ant?
  I can't
  Love an ant.
  I just can't."

"How about a bee
  With a lazy buzz?"

"No. I don't like honey
  And he does."

"Play with a cricket.
  Play with a quail.
  Tame you a lizard
  With a sandy tail."

"They're all good friends
  But they're just not boys
  And they can't make
  That fine boy-noise."

Amigo tried to make them understand.
"I'm as much a part of the desert land
   As any mountain or grain of sand,
   Or soft quail cry
   Or sunset sky
   Or dust-devil blowing high
   As a bird.
   And that boy
   Is a part of it too—
   The same as I.
   He's a desert thing like any other.
   Sometimes I think he is my brother."

   Amigo's mother nodded her head.
"Taming a boy seems odd," she said.
"It's never been done, as far as I know,
   But no one ever loved one so—
   And that makes all the difference.
   You may be the one
   Who will do it, my son."

"The thing to do now
   Is tame him.
   But how?
   What can I give him?
   I wish I knew.
   I have no treasures,
   Not even a few."

"Just give him something
That pleases you."

"Like silvery sand
  To hold in his hand?
  Or the blue jay feather
  That floated down
  Straight from the sky
  To Prairie-Dog Town?
  Or that cool green shadowy grass
  Which grows so tall at the mountain pass
  And tastes of mountain water?"

His mother said, "These
  Would surely please
  A boy."

So Amigo scampered
And ran and hopped.
The sun was high
Before he stopped—
At the very top
Of the mountain pass,
Where all the grass
Was sweet as honey
And tall enough to hide in.
Amigo took great pride in
His work that day.

He sniffed a thousand blades of grass
Before he found the one
That smelled the most like mountain water—
And shone like mountain sun.

He took the green blade
Tenderly down
Into the valley near
Prairie-Dog Town.
And beside the path
Where the boy often came,
He placed the grass on a small white stone—
Which he always thought of
As his own.

As he waited he made a kind of game
Of dreaming the boy was already tame
And knew his name—
And said,
"Amigo."

But it was no game,
For the boy came along
Trailing his song
In the windy air.
And it was no dream,
For he saw Amigo there.
He did not speak.
He only sat
Very quietly gazing at
The world of sun and sand.
And when he left, a blade of grass
Was clutched in his brown hand.

And Amigo ran home
Bounding with joy,
Shouting, "Listen,
I've just about
Tamed me a boy!"

At the same time,
On the same day,
You could hear
Francisco say,
"Mama, I know that he's
Just about mine!
Isn't that wonderful?
Isn't that fine?"

Francisco went back to the stone
Every day.
He was a friend
In every way.
He brought wild cherries
Gathered in the mountains
And fat dark berries
That grew on sandy banks.
To see Amigo eat them
Was all the thanks
He needed.
When the summer sun beat fiercely down
And the heat lay heavy on Prairie-Dog Town,
He found a rock shaped like a cup
And every morning he filled it up
With water.

And he kept one eye on the sky
To warn Amigo when hawks flew by.
And every day
Amigo came closer
To the place
Where Francisco sat—
As near as that.

The boy was taming Amigo.
Oh, yes,
That's so.
And if you were watching Amigo
You'd know
That he was taming Francisco.
And you would think
The boy wished he were tame
The way he came
Closer
And
Closer.

Francisco took the presents
Amigo left here and there.
He even stuck that blue jay
Feather in his hair.

Many a time
The boy would lie down
In the tall wispy grass
Near Prairie-Dog Town,
Quiet as a field mouse in its nest,
Like any desert creature taking a rest.
Amigo liked knowing that he was near.
He listened for his whistle in the summer air—
And sure enough the whistle was there!

Amigo ran
Close to the sound.
Francisco smiled,
Turned around
And met Amigo.

That was the way
It happened that day.
First they climbed a hill.
They followed a bee.
Then they stopped to rest
By a mesquite tree.
They didn't talk much for the wind was shrill.
They sat there quietly, as good friends will,
Admiring the view from that rocky hill.

Now
Francisco thought,
"I've tamed me a prairie dog.
He's my greatest joy."
And
Amigo thought,
"Mine is the *best* pet.
I've tamed me a boy."

Amigo squeaked a happy sound,
And when he was through
Francisco said, "Yes,
I think so too."

Meet the Author:
Byrd Baylor

Byrd Baylor lives in a desert very much like the desert in the story. The prairie dogs near her desert home gave Ms. Baylor the idea to write *Amigo*. One summer she was learning to make tortillas, which are round, flat pieces of bread. Because the tortillas weren't very good, no one would eat them. So, Ms. Baylor and her son fed them to the prairie dogs. The prairie dogs liked the tortillas very much. One day, the author found blue-jay feathers on the rock where the prairie dogs had eaten the tortillas. Later she found some beautiful stones on the same rock. Ms. Baylor thought the feathers and stones must have been gifts from the prairie dogs. She used this real event in her life to write her story *Amigo*.

Byrd Baylor has written other books about the desert and desert animals. You might want to read *The Desert Is Theirs* and *I'm in Charge of Celebrations*.

Responding to Literature

1. Think about a time when you wanted something of your own. Explain how your feelings were similar to or different from Francisco's.

2. If one of Francisco's friends asked him what he did to make friends with a desert animal, what would Francisco answer?

3. Francisco looks for a prairie dog. Amigo looks for a boy. How do Francisco and Amigo know they are friends at last?

4. Amigo is the first prairie dog Francisco has tamed, and Francisco is the first boy Amigo has tamed. Do you think Francisco or Amigo will want to tame another friend? Explain your answer.

5. A story can be told using words in different ways. *Amigo* is a long poem that tells a story. Do you think telling *Amigo* as a story poem makes it more fun to read? Tell why or why not.

Chums

He sits and begs, he gives a paw,
He is, as you can see,
The finest dog you ever saw,
And he belongs to me.

He follows everywhere I go
And even when I swim.
I laugh because he thinks, you know,
That I belong to him.

But still no matter what we do
We never have a fuss;
And so I guess it must be true
That *we* belong to *us*.

Arthur Guiterman

Finding Out About the Story

Thinking About Setting and Character

In *Amigo,* Byrd Baylor chose the desert as the setting of her story. Her two characters, Francisco and Amigo, become friends as they meet while sharing the same place to play. The author also shows you that Francisco and Amigo each feel the other is a perfect desert friend. Read what Amigo says about Francisco below.

"He's a desert thing like any other.
Sometimes I think he is my brother."

You can see why the desert setting is important to the story. It is the place where two characters meet, play, leave gifts for each other, and become friends.

Writing About Setting and Character

A desert is a perfect home for a prairie dog. Would Amigo be happy living where you do?

Prewriting On your own paper, answer the questions in the chart you see on the next page. Think about the reasons why the desert is a good place for Amigo. Decide why Amigo would or would not be happy where you live.

	In the desert	Where I live
1. Could Amigo run free?	Yes	
2. Could Amigo find food to eat?		
3. Could Amigo dig holes?		
4. Could Amigo live with his relatives?		

Writing Use the answers in the chart to help you write a paragraph that gives reasons why Amigo would be a good pet to keep where you live. Then write a paragraph that tells why Amigo would not be a good pet to keep where you live.

Revising Read your draft aloud to a partner. Ask your partner, "Did I include reasons why Amigo could and couldn't live where I do?" If you need to, revise your draft to include more than one reason. (For ideas about revising, turn to the Writer's Handbook.)

Presenting Share your paragraphs with a partner. Listen as your partner reads his or her paragraphs. Decide if it would be a good idea for you or your partner to keep Amigo for a pet.

Extending Your Reading

Expressing Yourself
Choose one or more of these activities:

Tape the Story Poem Take turns reading a part of *Amigo* with a partner. After you have practiced reading a part of the poem aloud, make a tape with your partner. Play your tape and have your classmates follow along in their books.

Make a Model Fill a shallow box with sand to make a desert setting. Make desert plants and animals from clay or paper to add to your model. If you like, include a prairie-dog town.

Find Something Special A blue-jay feather was special to Amigo. What special object from nature would you like to bring to school to show to your classmates? Make sure your object is not being used by any living thing.

Pick a Pet Francisco could have chosen a lizard or a tortoise for a pet. If you were Francisco, what animal would you have chosen? Discuss your choice with a group of classmates.

More Books About the Southwest

The Girl Who Loved Wild Horses by Paul Goble
A village girl has a special way with horses. During an earth-shaking thunderstorm, she is carried far from her village on the back of a frightened horse. The horse takes her to a place she has never been before.

Cactus in the Desert by Phyllis S. Busch
In some parts of the desert, it rains only once or twice a year. Yet some cactuses grow taller than ten people standing on each other's shoulders. Read more about these amazing plants.

Blue Canyon Horse by Ann Nolan Clark
Something wild calls a little mare in the nighttime. The little horse wants to run free with the wild horses. The Navajo boy who owns her does not understand why his horse wants to leave. If she does, will he ever see her again?

Roadrunner by Naomi John
The roadrunner is an unusual bird that lives in the desert. It likes to race with people as they drive by in their cars. Spend a day with this fast and funny bird.

Hear
the Music

Introducing

Hear the Music

What ways can you make music? Perhaps you can sing songs, dance to music, or listen to it. You might play an instrument to make music. Sometimes singing, dancing, or musical instruments can help tell a story. The music works together with the words of a story to tell something that happens.

Stories and Music

In 1936, a great composer named Prokofieff (prō kō′fi′ef) took a folk tale and put it to music. He had a narrator tell the story, and then instruments of an orchestra played music to sound like the characters in the story. That is the story of *Peter and the Wolf.* Hearing the music of the animals and people in the story helps the listener picture what happens.

In *The Sign on Rosie's Door,* Maurice Sendak wrote about a girl named Rosie who wants to be a great singing star. Rosie puts on her own show.

Rosie's show became a real play, put on in a theater in New York City. In an article, author Bill

Powers tells you how the play *Really Rosie* came to be. He shows you that a writer wrote a script with words for the actors to say. A choreographer (kôr′ē og′rə fər) planned dance steps and taught them to the actors. Then a director guided the actors as they rehearsed, or practiced, the play.

Types of Literature

Some stories are fantasies with make-believe characters who do make-believe things. Other stories are realistic, and are about people we *might* know. Both kinds of stories are called fiction. Nonfiction is a type of literature about real people and real events. In this section, you'll read fiction in a folk tale and a realistic story about children you might know. You'll also read a nonfiction article about real people. In each, music is important.

As you're reading on your own, discover how music is important in each selection.

Peter and the Wolf

by Serge Prokofieff

Each character of this tale is represented by a corresponding instrument in the orchestra:

Peter by the string quartet ,

the bird by the flute,

 the duck by
the oboe,

 the wolf by
three horns,

 the cat by the
clarinet in low
register,

 the shooting of
the hunters by
kettle and
bass drums.

 the grandfather
by the bassoon,

ANDANTINO

Early one morning Peter opened the gate and went out into the big green meadow. On the branch of a birch tree sat a little bird, Peter's friend. When he saw Peter he chirped at him gaily, "All's quiet here."

Soon a duck came waddling around. She was very happy to see that Peter had not closed the gate, and so decided to have a nice swim in the deep pond in the meadow.

L'ISTESSO TEMPO

mf espress.

L'ISTESSO TEMPO

mf espress.

293

As soon as the little bird saw the duck, he flew down and settled himself in the grass beside her. Shrugging his shoulders he said, "What kind of bird are *you* if you can't fly?" To which the duck replied, "What kind of a bird are *you* if you can't swim?" and dived into the pond.

They argued and argued, the duck swimming in the pond, the little bird hopping back and forth along the bank.

Suddenly something caught Peter's eye. It was a cat crawling through the grass. The cat said to herself, "The bird is busy arguing. If I could only have him for my dinner!"

MODERATO

con eleganza

Stealthily she crept toward him on her velvet paws. "Oh, look out!" cried Peter.

Quickly the bird flew up into the tree while the duck quacked angrily at the cat—from the middle of the pond. The cat crawled round and round the tree and thought, "Is it worth climbing up so high? By the time I get there the bird will have flown away."

POCO PIÙ ANDANTE

All at once Grandpapa came out. He was angry because Peter had gone to the meadow. "The meadow is a dangerous place," he cried. "What if a wolf should come out of the forest?—What would you do then?" Peter paid no attention to Grandpapa's words.

Boys like Peter are not afraid of wolves. Grandpapa took Peter by the hand, led him home, and locked the gate.

No sooner had Peter gone than a big grey wolf *did* come out of the forest.
In a twinkling the cat
sprang up into the tree.
The duck quacked and
in her great excitement,
jumped out of the pond.

No matter how hard the duck tried to run, she couldn't escape the wolf. He was getting nearer and nearer. He was catching up with her—there—he got her—and swallowed her with a single gulp!

And now this is how things stood: the cat was sitting on one branch up in the tree, the bird was sitting on another—not too close to the cat—while the wolf walked round and round the tree, looking at them both with greedy eyes. In the meantime, Peter, without the slightest fear, stood behind the closed gate, watching all that was going on. Presently,

he ran into the house, found a strong rope, hurried back and climbed up the high stone wall. One of the branches of the tree around which the wolf was pacing, stretched out over this high wall. Grabbing hold of this branch, Peter climbed over into the tree. He said to the bird, "Fly down and circle around the wolf's head, but take care that he doesn't catch you!" The bird almost touched the wolf's head with his wings, while the wolf snapped furiously at him from this side and that. How that bird did worry the wolf! And oh! how the wolf tried to catch him! But the bird was far too clever for him.

Meanwhile, Peter had made a lasso, and letting it down very carefully—he caught the wolf by the tail and pulled with all his might. Feeling himself caught, the wolf began to jump wildly, trying to get

loose. But Peter had tied the other end of the rope to the tree, and the wolf's jumping only made the rope tighter around his tail! Just then, who should come out

of the woods but the hunters who were following the wolf's trail, and shooting as they came. From his perch in the tree Peter cried out to them: "You don't need to shoot. The bird and I have already caught him! Please help us take him to the zoo."

The hunters were only too willing. And now you can just imagine the triumphant procession! Peter at the head—after him the hunters, leading the wolf—and winding up the procession, Grandpapa and the cat. Grandpapa shook his head reprovingly. "This is all very well, but what if Peter had *not* caught the wolf—what then!"

Above them flew the little bird, merrily chirping, "Aren't we smart, Peter and I? See what *we* have caught!" And if you had listened very carefully, you could have heard the duck quacking away inside the wolf, because in his haste the wolf had swallowed her whole—and the duck was still alive.

Meet the Composer:
Serge Prokofieff

From the time that he was a little boy, Serge Prokofieff loved music. He said that listening to his mother play the piano helped him to enjoy music when he was very young. Later, when Prokofieff was eleven years old, his first music teacher helped him to write his first piece of music for an orchestra to perform. When he grew up and became a famous musician, Prokofieff wanted to help children learn to appreciate music and the instruments in the orchestra. He wrote his musical folk tale *Peter and the Wolf,* to teach young listeners to recognize the instruments in an orchestra and the sounds they make. When Prokofieff wrote down his music for an orchestra to play, he included a note to musicians telling them that children should *see* and hear the instruments that stand for each character before *Peter and the Wolf* is performed. Prokofieff shared his love for music by writing other music for children, but *Peter and the Wolf* is his most popular work.

Responding to Literature

1. A filmmaker wants to make *Peter and the Wolf* into a movie. Do you think this is a good idea? Explain your answer.

2. Pretend that you are Peter. Tell what steps you took to capture the wolf.

3. One reader of *Peter and the Wolf* said that she thought having music explain the story was like having an extra set of illustrations. How is music important in the folk tale?

4. The composer of the music for *Peter and the Wolf* chose certain instruments to play the parts of different animals. Why did he choose a flute for the bird's part and three horns to play the wolf's part?

5. At the end of the folk tale, Grandpapa says, "This is all very well, but what if Peter had not caught the wolf—what then!" What do you think would have happened?

Oh, A-Hunting We Will Go

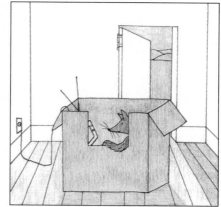

Oh, a-hunting we will go,
A-hunting we will go;
We'll catch a fox
And put him in a box,
And then we'll let him go!

We'll catch a lamb
And put him in a pram,
And then we'll let him go!

We'll catch a goat
And put him in a boat,
And then we'll let him go!

We'll catch a bear
And put him in underwear,
And then we'll let him go!

We'll catch a whale
And put him in a pail,
And then we'll let him go!

We'll catch a snake
And put him in a cake,
And then we'll let him go!

We'll catch a mouse
And put him in a house,
And then we'll let him go!

We'll catch a pig
And put him in a wig,
And then we'll let him go!

We'll catch a skunk
And put him in a bunk,
And then we'll let him go!

We'll catch an armadillo
And put him in a pillow,
And then we'll let him go!

We'll catch a fish
And put him in a dish,
And then we'll let him go!

We'll catch a brontosaurus
And put him in a chorus,
And then we'll let him go!

Oh, a-hunting we will go,
A-hunting we will go;
We'll just pretend and in
    the end,
We'll always let them go!

John Langstaff

The Sign on
Rosie's Door

Written and Illustrated by Maurice Sendak

There was a sign on Rosie's door.

It read, "If you want to know a secret, knock three times."

Kathy knocked three times and Rosie opened the door.

"Hello, Kathy."

"Hello, Rosie. What's the secret?"

"I'm not Rosie any more," said Rosie. "That's the secret."

"Then who are you?" asked Kathy.

"I'm Alinda, the lovely lady singer."

"Oh," said Kathy.

"And someday," said Rosie, "I'll sing in a great musical show."

"When?" Kathy asked.

"Now, in my back yard. Want to come?"

"Can I be somebody too?" asked Kathy.

Rosie had to think for a minute.

"I suppose," she said finally, "you can be Cha-Charoo, my Arabian dancing girl."

"All right," said Kathy. "I'll come."

And everybody came. Dolly and Pudgy and Sal.

"Now sit down everybody," Rosie said.

They all sat down on folding chairs.

"Now keep quiet everybody," said Rosie. "The show is going to begin."

They all sat quietly. Rosie and Kathy disappeared behind the cellar door.

"This is a good show," Pudgy whispered.

"It is," said Dolly.

BAM, BAM, BAM! came the sound of a drum from behind the cellar door.

"Ladies and gentlemen!" cried a faraway voice. "We have for your pleasure Cha-Charoo, the Arabian dancing girl. Clap and shout hooray!"

Everybody shouted and clapped. The cellar door opened and Kathy stepped out. She wore a nightgown and had a towel over her head. She waved her arms and took three little steps.

"Cha-Charoo-roo-roo," she sang softly.

"That's enough," cried the voice from behind the cellar door.

"Clap, everybody, and shout hooray!"

Clap. Clap. Clap!

"Hooray. Hooray. Hooray!"

"Now comes the best part of the show," the voice continued. "Me, Alinda, the lovely lady singer, who will sing for your pleasure 'On the Sunny Side of the Street.' Everybody say Oh and Ah!"

"Oh!"

"Ah!"

"Oh, ah!"

The cellar door opened and out came Alinda. She wore a hat with feathers sticking out, a lady's dress, and high-heeled shoes.

"Hello, everybody!" someone said.

Everybody turned and saw Lenny wearing a fireman's hat.

"Can I play too?" he asked.

"We're not playing," Alinda shouted. "It's a real show and you can't."

"Why?"

"Because."

"Anyway," said Lenny, "I have to go put out a fire. Everybody want to come?"

They all shook their heads no.

Lenny ran out of the yard.

"Now I'll sing," Alinda said.

She closed her eyes. "On the sun—"

"Want to know something?" asked Lenny.

He was back again.

"What?" asked Alinda.

"I know a trick," said Lenny.

"What trick?"

"First," Lenny explained, "I throw my fireman's hat up in the air and then the one who catches it can keep it. Everybody want to play?"

They all shook their heads yes.

"All right," said Alinda.

Lenny threw the hat high into the air and it landed on Rosie's window ledge.

"How will we catch it now?" Kathy asked.

"We'll have to climb up for it," said Alinda.

So they did. Sal climbed on top of Pudgy. Dolly climbed on top of Sal. Kathy on top of Dolly. Lenny on top of Kathy, and Alinda on top of everybody. She took the fireman's hat off the window ledge and put it on her head.

"I caught it, it's mine," she shouted. "Hooray for me!"

They all climbed down.

"Now I'll sing," Alinda said.

She stretched out her arms. "On the sun—"

"Give me back my hat," said Lenny. "I have to go put out another fire."

"No," said Alinda. "You said for keeps."

"It was only a game," said Lenny, "and my mother says I shouldn't give anything away any more."

He pulled the hat off Alinda's head and ran out of the yard.

"Come on, Pudgy," he called. "Come on, Sal, help me put the fire out!"

"We better help him," said Pudgy.

"He needs us," said Sal.

"But—" Alinda began.

But they were already gone.

"I better go too," said Dolly.

"I didn't sing my song yet," said Alinda.

"I'm hungry," Dolly answered. And she went home.

They were all gone. Two of the folding chairs lay on their sides.

"It's getting late," said Kathy. "I have to go home."

"Wasn't it a wonderful show?" asked Rosie.

"It was the best I ever saw," Kathy answered. "Let's have another one soon."

"Same time, same place," said Rosie.

"Good-by, Cha-Charoo."

"Good-by, Alinda."

Rosie was all alone. She climbed on top of a folding chair and said very quietly, "Ladies and gentlemen, Alinda will now sing 'On the Sunny Side of the Street.' "

And she sang the song all the way to the end.

Meet the Author and Illustrator: **Maurice Sendak**

The made-up character Rosie is based on a real person whom Maurice Sendak never met but would watch from his window overlooking a Brooklyn street. He enjoyed watching Rosie playing her make-believe games. Mr. Sendak liked Rosie because she could "imagine herself into being anything she wanted to be, anywhere in or out of the world."

The author liked Rosie so much that all of the young characters he wrote books about later have Rosie's energetic personality. Maurice Sendak has received many awards for the books he has written and illustrated. You may want to reread his famous book *Where the Wild Things Are.*

Responding to Literature

1. Rosie is a character who makes people notice her. What do you like most about Rosie? What do you like least?

2. As Rosie finds out, sometimes even the biggest stars lose the audience's attention. What are the events that happen to cause Rosie to "lose" her audience?

3. Rosie likes to dress up and pretend that she isn't Rosie anymore. She also likes to entertain her friends. How is music important to Rosie?

4. No one stays to listen to Rosie sing her song, "On the Sunny Side of the Street." Why would Rosie sing her song even though no one listens?

Behind the Scenes
of a Broadway Musical

Written and Photographed
by Bill Powers

Nine young actors were lined up on the stage, their faces stretched in grins, top hats waving in the air. The opening night audience in the packed theater was grinning back, clapping in time to the music. The cast bowed and the audience burst into applause. The first performance of Maurice Sendak's *Really Rosie* was over. After all the hard work it seemed like a magic moment. The cast stood erect again, looked at each other and smiled, and bowed again.

Five weeks earlier, the warm lights that lit the actors' faces were still on the shelves. The colorful scenery that surrounded the actors did not exist. Neither did the costumes they wore nor the top hats they were waving above their heads. Five weeks earlier, the stage they were standing on was an empty space.

Really Rosie tells the story of how a group of kids on a Brooklyn street spend a hot, boring summer day. With nothing to do, they look to Rosie to entertain them. Rosie has a dream of becoming a movie star and makes up the plot of a movie about her rise to stardom—and her search for her long-lost brother, Chicken Soup (who is really not lost, but hiding in a

The young actors in Really Rosie *listen to the applause at the end of their performance.*

large cardboard box). All the kids audition for her movie as Rosie relates the story of Chicken Soup's disappearance, and at the end of the play, Rosie rewards them all with parts in the "movie of her life."

The first musical version of *Really Rosie* was presented as an animated cartoon TV special in 1975, based on Maurice Sendak's children's book *The Sign on Rosie's Door* and the four volumes in his *Nutshell Library*. The music was written by Carole King, with lyrics by Sendak. This time the musical would be done with live actors in New York, and would be directed by Pat Birch.

Planning the Play

While work begins on the scenery, lighting, and costumes, the director and choreographer hold auditions for the singers and dancers trying out for parts in the play. For *Really Rosie* the dancing was not as important as the singing and acting, so during auditions the emphasis was on finding young actors who could sing well. Pat Birch would teach them what little dancing there was to learn.

Auditions are a little like a contest. The actor will usually sing a song he or she has been practicing as an audition piece. If the director and the others like what they hear, the actor will then be asked to read a part of the script. If the actor reads well, the director might give him or her one of the songs from the show to take home and learn and the actor would be given a "callback." This can happen again and again until the actor either gets the part or is let go.

In the auditions, the director is not just trying to find talented actors and singers, but actors whose looks and personalities fit the characters in the play and who are talented enough to make the play come to life on the stage.

Tisha Campbell auditions for a part in the play.

 323

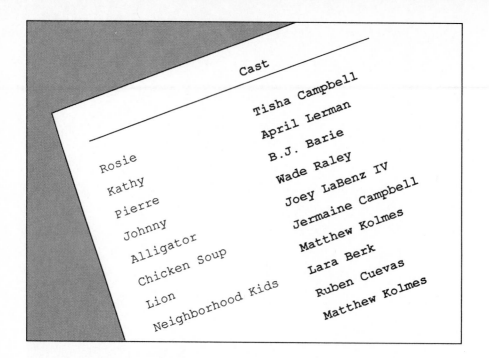

Cast

Rosie	Tisha Campbell
Kathy	April Lerman
Pierre	B.J. Barie
Johnny	Wade Raley
Alligator	Joey LaBenz IV
Chicken Soup	Jermaine Campbell
Lion	Matthew Kolmes
Neighborhood Kids	Lara Berk
	Ruben Cuevas
	Matthew Kolmes

Rehearsals Begin

It looks like fun and sometimes it is, but rehearsing a play is mostly hard work. And in a professional production like *Really Rosie*, that is what the actors are paid for—hard work. The usual work week for a play is eight hours a day, six days a week, plus the homework of learning lines and studying the play. Because of their ages and the fact that they would have to miss school during the weeks of rehearsal, a tutor would come in and help each of the cast keep up with schoolwork.

In working on a play, memorizing the lines and learning the songs is the easy part. Almost anyone can do it. An actor's primary job in rehearsal is to create an interesting character and to bring to life the role he or she has been assigned to play.

After the first week of rehearsals, an actor usually knows all of his or her lines and songs and no longer has to carry a script on stage. It is then that the real work on the part can begin. Pat Birch, the director, and Tisha Campbell, who played Rosie, spent hours and hours just on Rosie's first speech in the play. Rosie is the main character. It is Rosie who helps the other kids on the street get through the long summer day. It is Rosie who must set the tone of the play. In her first speech and song, Rosie has to catch the audience's attention and get them interested—because if Rosie can't, the rest of the play will be in trouble.

The Music

The entire cast of *Really Rosie* was made up of very young actors, most of whom could not read music. They had to learn the songs by ear. To speed up the process, the musical director, Joel Silberman, used the following technique during the first week of rehearsals to help Wade Raley, one of the actors, learn his long solo in "One Was Johnny."

Joel sang while Wade listened and followed the lyrics in his script. Then Wade sang with Joel guiding him through the song. Next, Joel sang a short section and Wade repeated it. They went through the entire song this way. Then Joel made a tape of Wade singing so Wade could take it home and study it.

A few days later, when Wade was sure of the lyrics, another tape was made. This time Wade and Joel sang together. The purpose of the new tape was to help Wade hit the proper notes. This method was used only

Joel Silberman, the musical director, works with the cast on a song.

for the solos. When the entire cast sang, Joel had to
teach them their parts during rehearsal, which meant a
lot of time at the piano.

Really Rosie used a small backstage band of five
musicians, including Joel, who conducted from the
piano. The five musicians played a total of nine
instruments.

Using the songs in the show, Joel also had to
compose an overture, which is the music played just
before the curtain rises and the show begins. The
overture is meant to reflect the spirit of the play and
put the audience in the right mood.

Previews

Previews are performances that are used to test a play in front of a paying audience. They tell if the play works as planned, what changes would make it better, and, more important, whether the audience likes it or not.

The first preview of *Really Rosie* was on the night of October 2. Almost every day after that, rehearsals were held before each performance to correct what went wrong the night before. This didn't end until opening night.

At some point in the rehearsal period, during a run-through or later during the previews, it suddenly happens. The actors take over the play. They take the play out of the hands of the playwright and the

The cast sings and dances in a performance of Really Rosie.

composer, and the director who has guided them, and make it theirs. This has to happen if a show is to be successful. The performers on stage are the ones the audience sees. The words they speak and the songs they sing must sound like their words, their songs, not something they were taught. The action on stage has to seem like it is happening for the first time. And, in a good production of a good play, it always does.

It happened in *Really Rosie* during the second week of previews. When Pat Birch gathered the cast in the front row after the performance on October 12, she said, "It was a good show. I have a few notes, but I'll give them tomorrow." She looked up and down the line and added, "The show is yours."

Opening Night

Janet, the stage manager, looked at her watch and called out into the theater to the house manager. "Okay, you can open the house." Customers trickled in as Janet went to the backstage mike. "Fifteen minutes, please. Fifteen minutes." The band continued to rehearse as Janet made a final backstage inspection to be sure all the props were in their correct places.

Everyone was ready. The boys heard Janet's voice over the loudspeaker. "Five minutes, please. Five minutes." The boys tumbled out of the dressing room to join the girls and their director. They joined hands and Pat Birch gave them some words of encouragement and a gentle warning. "Remember, if you make a mistake, don't worry about it. Once it's done, go on. You can't fix it. So don't try. Just go on." The kids nodded. "Now go out there and knock their blocks off."

Janet interrupted them. "Places. Let's go, kids. Places." The actors moved out to take their positions on either side of the stage. Pat hurried to her seat in the audience. The band was warming up.

"Ladies and gentlemen, boys and girls, welcome to *Really Rosie.*" As the house lights dimmed, the band swung into the overture.

As the end of the overture approached, Tisha got into position and straightened her dress. Stagehands reached up and grabbed the curtain rope. Tisha stood

poised. The stagehands hauled up the curtain. A golden light bathed Tisha as she stepped forward to greet it. Tisha stood downcenter, spread her arms and began to sing, "I'm really Rosie . . . ."

And she really was.

Meet the Author and Photographer:
Bill Powers

Bill Powers is both an author and a photographer. In addition to writing *Behind the Scenes of a Broadway Musical,* he also took the photographs. Mr. Powers's other photographs have appeared in many other books and magazines. He has written other books for children and has illustrated books that other authors have written.

Putting on a play is something Bill Powers knows how to do too. He started an acting group called the "Second Story Players" and also directed the group. His Second Story Players won an important theater award called the Obie Award.

Responding to Literature

1. *Behind the Scenes of a Broadway Musical* tells you many facts about how real actors get ready to perform a musical show. From what you've learned by reading the article, what do you think would be the most exciting part about being in a play?

2. The actors in *Really Rosie* work hard to be able to perform in the play on opening night. Tell what the actors have to learn and do before the first performance of *Really Rosie.*

3. The lights that brighten the stage, the costumes that actors wear, and the lines that they must learn are important in putting on a play. How is music important to a play?

4. Singers, musicians, a composer, and a musical director all work together to put on a Broadway musical. If you chose to have one of those jobs, what would you need to know to do the job?

I Am Rose

I am Rose my eyes are blue
I am Rose and who are you?
I am Rose and when I sing
I am Rose like anything.

From a poem by Gertrude Stein

Finding Out About Types of Literature

Thinking About Fiction and Nonfiction

Authors choose different ways to tell their stories. Prokofieff used music and a narrator to tell a folk tale. Maurice Sendak wrote a story about a made-up character named Rosie who likes to sing. Bill Powers wrote an article about real people putting on a musical play about Rosie.

The Sign on Rosie's Door and *Peter and the Wolf* are types of writing called fiction. Fiction is writing that comes mostly from the author's imagination. Bill Powers's article is nonfiction. Nonfiction is writing that gives facts about real people, places, things, or events. The article tells how a musical play about Rosie came to be.

Even though the types of literature are different in the way they're written, each shows you how music can be used to help tell a story.

Writing a Story

Create and name your own special character. Make up a story about him or her.

Prewriting Draw two stars similar to the one on page 335. Next to each star, write what Rosie and Peter want and what each does to get it.

Next draw a third star for your own character. Write what your character wants and what he or she does to get it. (For ideas about writing, turn to the Handbook.)

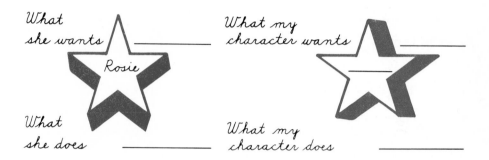

Writing Write a story about your character. Tell what your character wants and how he or she does something to reach that goal. Include where your story takes place. Add an interesting title.

Revising Read your draft to a partner. Ask, "Does my story tell how my character reaches a goal?" If you need to, make changes to tell more about your character.

Presenting After you have read your story to a few friends, ask them to pretend to be the characters and act out the story. Present the story play for the class. If you choose, play some background music as you present the story.

Extending Your Reading

Expressing Yourself
Choose one or more of these activities:

Listen to "Peter and the Wolf" After reading the story of Peter and the Wolf, listen to the music that Prokofieff wrote for the fairy tale. Close your eyes and listen to how the instruments tell the story.

Make a Play Poster Make a big, colorful poster to advertise *Peter and the Wolf,* the musical story. Be sure to include the title and the author's name. Write a "catchy" phrase that will get people's attention.

Teach Your Favorite Song Teach a song to your classmates. If you don't want to sing alone, ask a partner or friends to join you. You might want to bring in a recording of the song to play for the class as they sing.

Show Your Talent Participate in a "Talent Day." Tell and show your classmates what you can do. You may bring in, and talk about, photographs you've taken, a musical instrument you play, or a trophy you've won.

More Books About Music

Really Rosie by Maurice Sendak
In this play to act out, Rosie decides to make a movie about her life. She isn't sure, however, which of her friends should be in the movie. Rosie spends the day listening to them sing and watching them dance. Who will Rosie choose to perform in her movie?

Georgia Music by Helen V. Griffith
After a move from Georgia to Baltimore to live with his daughter and granddaughter, Granddaddy misses the music made by the crickets and grasshoppers. He no longer plays tunes on his mouth organ as his granddaughter sings along. Find out what she does to help him hear that music again.

The Boy Who Loved Music by Joe Lasker
Winter is coming and Karl, who plays in the Prince's orchestra, can't leave the summer palace until the Prince does. The Prince's composer, Joseph Haydn, uses music in an unusual way to convince the Prince that it is time to go home.

From
Anna

by Jean Little

Illustrated by Nobee Kanayama

Introducing

From
Anna

   Suppose someone asked you, "What was one of the hardest things you've ever tried to do?" Think of something difficult, something that was a challenge. A girl named Anna, in the story *From Anna,* might say her biggest challenge is not to be Awkward Anna anymore. She just wants to be Anna, the best Anna she can be.

A New Life in a New Land
   From the time Anna Solden was born, she lived in the European country of Germany with Papa, Mama, and her older brothers and sisters, Rudi, Fritz, Gretchen, and Frieda. In the year 1933, Anna's family left Germany to begin a new life in Canada. Until Papa began teaching them English, Anna and her family spoke only the German language. In their new country, the Solden family faces the difficulties of speaking a new language. Anna must face these problems and more. Anna has trouble seeing the letters that spell the language of her new country. Even German words wriggle and blur before her eyes.

Because Anna's vision is so poor, the world around her looks cloudy and unclear, which makes it difficult for Anna to run and play and to read and write. Things just aren't as easy to do as she wishes they would be. Anna's new eyeglasses have helped her see better, but she must go to a special school to make schoolwork easier for her. Anna wonders what to expect at her new school, and she wonders what her new teacher will expect from her.

Anna Learns About Herself

Jean Little, the author of *From Anna,* chooses to show you how Anna feels about herself and how those feelings change. As the author shows you what Anna thinks and feels, you'll learn what the whole story is all about.

As you're reading this part of the book on your own, find out what Anna discovers about herself.

From Anna

Anna Solden is getting ready for her first day at her new school. Mama and Dr. Schumacher, the doctor who helped Anna get her new glasses, will be taking her to meet her new English-speaking teacher and classmates. Anna's father has been teaching her English, but school, and especially reading, have never been easy for Anna. Will school in this strange, new country be even more difficult?

☙ The Beginning ☙

"Anna, hurry," Mama called.

Anna pulled up her other long brown stocking and hooked it onto the suspenders which hung from a harness that went over her shoulders. She reached for the cotton petticoat Mama had put ready. Already she was too hot. She felt smothered in clothes. First there was the underwear which came down to her knees, then the straps holding up her suspenders, then the hateful, itchy ribbed stockings and now the petticoat.

Mama pushed aside the curtain that hung across the end of Anna's alcove. "Hurry up," she urged again.

Anna put on her white blouse and buttoned it. It gaped open between the buttons.

Mama sighed. "You grow so fast," she said.

Anna sighed too. She would stop growing if she knew how. She felt far too big already. Her heart lightened, though, as she stretched out her hand for her new tunic.

"One new thing each to start school in," Papa had decided.

Always before, they had whole new outfits for the first day of school, but by now they were getting used to things being different.

Gretchen had chosen a yellow blouse which made her fair hair shine like gold. The boys picked corduroy pants. When they got home, they pranced around in them, making them squeak. For once, Rudi was as silly as Fritz. Frieda and Anna got tunics.

"I hate it," Frieda had stormed. "It's dull and awful. Like a uniform!"

"It looks fine on you," Mama had insisted, ignoring the bright, more expensive dresses. "There is a good big hem to let down and it's serge too. It will last forever."

At that, Frieda moaned as though Mama had plunged a knife into her.

Anna loved her tunic, though. She liked running her fingers down the sharp pleats. She even liked the plainness of it. It *was* like a uniform. Anna had always secretly wanted a uniform.

"Sit up," Mama said now, "while I fix your hair."

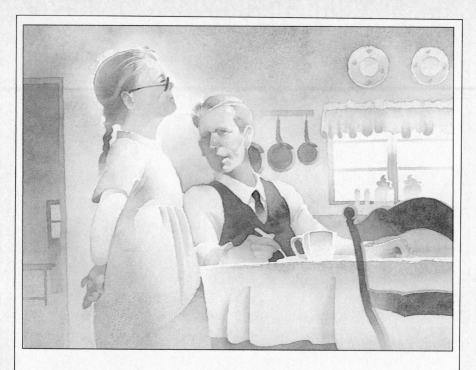

When it was done, she sent Anna to show herself to Papa.

Anna hurried until she reached the landing. The rest of the way she walked sedately, for she felt special-looking and grand. She presented herself proudly to her father.

Papa looked at her. Anna waited.

"Klara," he called, "what about ribbons for her hair?"

Anna stood as straight as before but the proud feeling inside her crumpled. She knew what Mama would say. Mama arrived and said it.

"Ribbons will not stay on Anna's hair," Mama said grimly. "However I will try again. Gretchen, run and get your new plaid ribbons."

When Dr. Schumacher arrived to take Mama and her to the new school, Anna was ready with a bright bow on each of her thin braids.

"You look lovely, Anna," the doctor smiled.

Anna looked away. She knew better.

"It is so kind of you to take Anna to this school," Mama fussed, getting herself and Anna into their coats.

"Nonsense," Dr. Schumacher said, "I know Miss Williams. I can help with the English, too. It won't take long."

The three of them found nothing to say to each other as they rode along. When they got out in front of the school, Anna marched along between her mother and the doctor. She tried to look as though this were something she did every day, as though her heart were not thudding so hard against her ribs it almost hurt. Franz Schumacher reached down his big warm hand and gathered up her cold little paw. Anna tried to jerk away but he held on. She gulped and went on walking: one foot . . . the other foot. His hand felt just like Papa's. She left her hand where it was and felt braver.

Miss Williams was the first surprise in what was to be a day of surprises.

"It's lovely to have you with us, Anna," she said when Dr. Schumacher drew Anna forward and introduced her and Mama.

The teacher had a low husky voice, not a bit like Frau Schmidt's. And her smile was so honest that even Anna could not doubt she meant it. She was pretty, too. Her hair was as bright as Gretchen's. She looked at Anna almost the way Papa did.

She doesn't know me yet, Anna reminded herself, not smiling in return. She hasn't heard me read.

"I've brought you a real challenge this time, Eileen," Dr. Schumacher said in an undertone.

Challenge.

Anna did not know that word. Did it mean "stupid one"? But no, it couldn't. Franz Schumacher still had her hand in his and the kindness of his grasp had not changed as he said it. Anna kept the new word in her mind. When she got home, she would ask Papa.

Fifteen minutes later she sat in her new desk and watched her mother and Dr. Schumacher leave the classroom.

"Don't leave me!" Anna almost cried out after them, her courage deserting her.

Instead, she put one hand up to feel the crispness of Gretchen's hair ribbon. One of the bows was gone. Anna pulled off the other one and shoved it out of sight into the desk.

She must not cry. She must *not!*

Then the desk itself caught her attention and distracted her. She had never seen one like it before. It had hinges on the sides and you could tip it up so that your book was close to you. She looked around wonderingly. The desk was not the only thing that was different. The pencil in the trough was bigger around than her thumb. The blackboards weren't black at all—they were green; and the chalk was fat too, and yellow instead of white.

Even the children were different. Most of them were older than Anna.

"We have Grades One to Seven in this room," Miss Williams had explained to Mama.

The desks were not set in straight rows nailed to the floor. They were pushed into separate groups. Miss Williams put Anna in one right beside her own desk near the front.

"You can sit next to Benjamin," she said. "Ben's been needing someone to keep him on his toes, haven't you, Ben?"

Anna had no idea how she was supposed to keep Benjamin on his toes. She looked sideways at his feet. They seemed perfectly ordinary.

Was it a joke, maybe?

Anna did not smile. It did not sound like a joke to her.

Quickly, Miss Williams told the new girl the names of all the other children in the class: Jane, Mavis, Kenneth, Bernard, Isobel, Jimmy, Veronica,

Josie, Charles. The names flew around Anna's ears like birds, each escaping just as she thought she had it safely captured.

"You won't remember most of them now," the teacher said, seeing panic in the child's eyes. "You'll have to get to know us bit by bit. Bernard is the oldest, so you'll soon know him because he runs us all."

Like Rudi, Anna said to herself. She would keep out of Bernard's way, if she could. Only she wasn't sure which one he was.

"I think you and Ben will probably be working together," Miss Williams went on.

"Introduce her to Ben properly, Miss Williams," a tall boy, who might be Bernard, suggested.

"Anna, allow me to present Benjamin Nathaniel Goodenough," Miss Williams obliged.

Anna stared at the small boy with black tufty hair and an impish face. He was a good head shorter than she was, though his glasses were as big as hers. Behind them, his eyes sparkled.

"I'm named after both my grandfathers," he explained.

"Now you know us well enough to begin with," the teacher said. "It's time we got some work done in this room."

Anna, who had been relaxed studying Benjamin Nathaniel, froze. What now? Would she have to read? She sat as still as a trapped animal while Miss Williams went to a corner cupboard. In a moment, she was back.

"Here are some crayons, Anna," she said. "I'd like

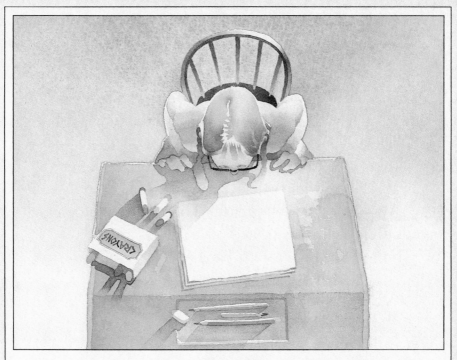

you to draw a picture. Anything you like. I'll get the
others started and then I'll be free to find out where
you are in your schoolwork."

Anna did not take the crayons. She did not know
anything she could draw. She was nowhere in her
schoolwork. She wanted Papa desperately.

And what did "challenge" mean?

"Draw your family, Anna," Miss Williams said.

She spoke with great gentleness but firmly too, as
though she knew, better than Anna did, what the
girl could do. She picked up one of Anna's square,
stubby hands and closed Anna's fingers around the
crayon box.

"Draw your father and your mother, your brothers
and your sisters—and yourself, too, Anna. I want to
see all of you."

The feel of the box, solid and real, brought back
Anna's courage. The crayons were big and bright.

They looked inviting. The teacher put paper on the desk, rough, cream-colored paper. Lovely paper for drawing. Six pieces, at least!

"Take your time," Miss Williams said, moving away. "Use as much paper as you need."

Anna took a deep breath. Then slowly she picked out a crayon. She knew how to start, anyway.

She would begin with Papa.

❧ A Challenge ❧

Anna made Papa extra tall. The top of his head touched the edge of the paper. She gave him wide shoulders and a big smile. She made his eyes very blue.

Then she put Mama next to him, holding his arm. Mama came up to his shoulder. Papa often joked about how small Mama was. He could rest his chin on top of her head.

Anna gave Mama a smile too but her crayon slipped as she did it and Mama's smile was crooked. Anna tried to fix it. She scratched at the wax with her fingernail. It flaked off but it left a smeary mark.

Should she start all over again—or give up?

Anna looked down at Papa, so tall, so happy. She drew a new smile on Mama's face over the place where the crooked one had been. This time the smile was fine but you could still see where she had made the mistake.

I know, Anna thought with sudden excitement. I'll make her sunburned and cover it up.

Carefully, she colored in the rest of Mama's face till it was rosy right up to her hair. It worked.

They've been on a holiday, Anna told herself, smiling a little at last. She made Papa's face match.

She paused and thought. By now she had forgotten the rest of the class. Her eyes lighted and she bent over her drawing once more.

She put Fritz's pail in Papa's hand. It didn't show, but Anna knew there was a little fish inside that pail.

Next she put in Rudi and Gretchen. They, too, were tall and sunburned. They had bright yellow hair and bright blue eyes. They had bathing suits on. Rudi was carrying his butterfly net. It was new and he was proud of it. Gretchen had Frieda's pail, full of seashells. The two of them were walking along beside Papa.

The twins took up most of the space next to Mama. They were running, their legs kicking up. Fritz's ears stuck out like cup handles. They both looked much too lively to be carrying their own pails. Anna left them in bare feet.

She colored light brown sand in a band at the bottom of the page.

There. It's done, she told the part of herself that was just watching.

Then she remembered. "And yourself, too, Anna," Miss Williams had said.

There was still a little room left on the page at one side. She made herself fit into the small space. She made her hair plain brown, her eyes an ordinary blue. Wanting somehow to look as interesting as the rest, she tried to draw herself in her new tunic. But she could not make the pleats look like pleats. When she had done her best, the girl on the paper looked squinched up and ugly.

"I've spoiled it," mourned Anna. She closed the crayon box.

Miss Williams came and bent above her.

"Who are they, Anna?" she asked.

Slowly Anna began to explain in German.

Miss Williams did not stop her and tell her to talk English instead, but when Anna pointed and said *"Mein Papa,"* the teacher answered "Your father. My, he is tall, isn't he?"

"Yes," Anna replied in English, only half aware she was switching. She was too intent on making sure Miss Williams understood about the holiday.

"They are gone on . . . to the sea," she fumbled, looking in vain for an English word for "holiday."

"I thought they had," Miss Williams said.

It was not such a terrible day. Not once did the teacher ask Anna to read from a book. She printed the story of Anna's picture on another piece of paper. The letters were large and black. Anna read each line as it appeared. She did not panic. She did not think of this as reading.

Here is Anna's father.
He is big. He is happy.
Anna's mother is here too.
She is small. She is happy too.
They are at the sea.
Gretchen is Anna's big sister.
Rudi is Anna's big brother.
Gretchen and Rudi are happy at the sea.
Frieda is Anna's other sister.
Fritz is Anna's brother too.
Fritz and Frieda are twins.
The twins are happy here too.
Anna is in our class.
Our class is happy Anna is here.

"You like drawing, don't you, Anna," Miss
Williams said, picking up the picture and looking at
it again, smiling at the bright colors, the liveliness of
the twins.

Anna did not answer. She was too startled, even if
she had known what to say. She had always hated
drawing in school. Frau Schmidt would put a picture
of a tulip up on the board for them to draw. Once,
as a special treat, she had brought real flowers in a
vase. The others had been pleased with their pictures
that day, but in Anna's, the flowers had looked like
cabbages on sticks.

"Really, Anna!" Frau Schmidt had said.

Making this portrait of her family, Anna had forgotten that. This had not seemed the same thing at all.

She was still sitting with her mouth ajar when
Miss Williams went on to say something else,

something so much more surprising that Anna had to pinch herself to make sure she was not inventing the whole thing.

"You like reading, too. I can see that. And your English! I can hardly believe you've been in Canada such a short time. You are amazing, Anna."

Miss Williams was not nearly as amazed as Anna Elisabeth Solden. She, Anna, like reading!

She wanted to laugh but she did not. She still did not even smile openly.

All the same, Anna felt something happening deep inside herself, something warm and alive. She was happy.

She was also muddled. She did not know how to behave. She had never felt this way before, not in school anyway. She sat perfectly still, her plain face as stern as usual. Only her eyes, blinking behind the big new glasses, betrayed her uncertainty.

The teacher did not wait for an answer to the astonishing things she had said. She took the picture and the story and tacked them up on the bulletin board where the whole class could see them. Then she got Benjamin to come over and read the words aloud.

"Twins!" Ben said, his eyes sparkling with interest. "Wow!"

Anna sat and listened to other classes working. She learned about explorers with the boys and girls in Grade Five. Miss Williams did not seem to mind other children listening and learning.

After lunch the teacher wound up the Gramophone and put on a record.

"Get comfortable, everybody," she said, "so you can really hear this."

Another strange word! Anna waited and watched.

Ben sat on the floor, leaning his back against Miss Williams' desk. The boy Anna thought might be Bernard slid down in his seat till all you could see was his head. Mavis put her head down on her folded arms. Everybody relaxed, sprawled, slouched, leaned.

Anna settled herself a little more squarely on her chair. She did not slump or get down on the floor.

But I am comfortable, she told herself.

She stopped worrying about losing Gretchen's hair ribbon, about Miss Williams finding out how stupid she was at schoolwork. She listened with her whole self.

Music, cool quiet music, rippled through the room.

"What did this make you think of?" Miss Williams asked when the record finished.

"Rain," Isobel said. She was in Grade Four and had fat bouncy ringlets.

"I think water maybe," Ben tried.

"Rain's water," Isobel grinned at him.

"No, I mean water like a stream," Ben insisted, staying serious in spite of her.

"What do you think, Anna?" Miss Williams asked.

Anna blushed. She had not been going to say.

"I know that music from my home," she explained. "I know the name."

"Tell us," Miss Williams smiled.

"It is 'The Shine of the Moon,' " Anna stumbled. "But . . . ."

She stopped short. Miss Williams waited. The others waited too. All the faces turned toward Anna were friendly faces. She took a deep breath and finished.

"I think it is like rain too," she said.

"The record is 'The Moonlight Sonata' by Beethoven," Miss Williams said. "But Beethoven did not name it that. He could have been thinking of rain."

"Or a stream," Ben said stubbornly.

"Or a stream—or something else entirely," the teacher said. "Each of you, listening, will hear it differently. That's fine. That's what your imaginations are for—to use. Beethoven was a great composer. He was German—like Anna."

Anna held her head up at that. She and Beethoven!

Arithmetic was not hard. Numbers, in this classroom, were big and clear and they stayed still when you looked at them.

"Good work, Anna," Miss Williams said, looking over her shoulder.

Not, "Nobody would ever guess you were Gretchen Solden's sister!"

She doesn't even know Gretchen, Anna realized suddenly. She doesn't know any of them but me.

She felt lost for a moment. Her teachers had always known her family too. Then she sat straighter.

Just me, she told herself again.

Whatever this teacher thought of her, it would be because of what she, Anna, did or failed to do. It was a startling idea. Anna was not sure she liked it. She shoved it away in the back of her mind and went on with her arithmetic. But she did not forget.

When school was over, she walked past her own house and went on to the store where Papa was hard

at work. She waited off to one side. When the customers were gone, she stepped up and leaned on the counter.

"How did it go in school, my little one?" he asked hopefully.

Anna knew what he hoped but she ignored his question.

"Papa, what is a challenge?" She had said the word over and over to herself all day long so she would be able to ask.

Papa scratched his head.

"A challenge," he repeated. "Well, it is . . . something to be won, maybe. Something special that makes you try hard to win it."

Anna thought that over.

"Thank you, Papa," she said, turning away.

"But school," her father cried after her. "Tell me about it."

"It was fine," Anna said over her shoulder. Then she twirled around unexpectedly and gave him one of her rare half-smiles.

"It was a challenge," she said.

"Something special," she repeated, as she started for home. "Dr. Schumacher thinks I am something special . . . like Papa said . . . . But why something to be won?"

She gave a little hop all at once. She would not mind going back tomorrow.

"It is a challenge," she said over again, aloud, in English, to the empty street.

She liked that word.

Meet the Author: **Jean Little**

Jean Little understands Anna's problems very well. When the author was born, she couldn't see at all. As a little girl her vision improved, but her sight was still very poor. Ms. Little says she was very lucky to have parents who read to her and taught her to read before she was old enough to go to school.

Sometimes Jean Little was teased at school, as Anna was. Ms. Little says that going to the library helped her feel better. A librarian who knew her as a child said Ms. Little actually read every book on the library's shelves! The author says she is glad she spent so much time reading. It helped her become the writer she is today.

Responding to Literature

1. When people read stories, they often find a favorite part that they would like to remember or share. What is your favorite part of the story? Tell why it is your favorite.

2. Anna's father asks her, "How did it go in school, my little one?" Anna answers, "It was fine." Pretend you are Anna and tell him what happened.

3. Anna surprises her teacher, and herself, by showing what she can do. What does Anna discover about herself?

4. Anna learns that it is sometimes hard just being yourself. Why was it hard for Anna to think of herself as special?

By Myself

When I'm by myself
And I close my eyes
I'm a twin
I'm a dimple in a chin
I'm a room full of toys
I'm a squeaky noise
I'm a gospel song
I'm a gong
I'm a leaf turning red
I'm a loaf of brown bread
I'm a whatever I want to be
An anything I care to be
And when I open my eyes
What I care to be
Is me.

Eloise Greenfield

Finding Out About the Story

Thinking About Character and Theme

In *From Anna,* Jean Little writes about a character who changes her feelings about herself. At first, when Anna is asked to read, she thinks, "I can't." Then Anna's new teacher helps Anna change the way she thinks about herself. On the first day of school, Anna reads a story and finds out that she *likes* to read.

If someone asked you what the story is all about, which of these ideas would you choose?

> The story is all about how Anna learns to like reading.
>
> The story is all about how Anna learns to feel good about herself.

The first idea is only partly right. Although it's true that Anna learns to like reading, Ms. Little wants you to see what this means to Anna. She shows you that the story is all about how Anna learns to feel good about herself when Ms. Little writes, "All the same, Anna felt something happening deep inside herself, something warm and alive. She was happy."

Writing About Character and Theme

Write about something that you did and why it makes you feel proud of yourself.

Prewriting On your own paper, write what Anna did that made her feel proud. Then write what you have done that makes you feel proud.

	Anna	Me
Proud	that she read a story	

Writing Start a journal, which is a book that tells of events that happen to you. Choose one event that made you feel proud. Write a paragraph about it for your journal. Describe what you did and why that makes you feel proud.

Revising Read your draft to yourself. Did you include reasons why you feel proud? If you need to, make changes so your paragraph gives reasons why you feel good about yourself. (For ideas about revising, turn to the Handbook.)

Presenting Reread your paragraph and put it in a folder with the title "My Journal." Keep adding new pages to your journal by writing about other events as they happen to you.

Extending Your Reading

Expressing Yourself
Choose one or more of these activities:

"Talk" Without Words Pretend that you are taking a trip to a country where people speak another language, such as Germany, where Anna lived. How would you make the people in that country understand you? In a small group, try to communicate a message without using words.

Draw Your Family Make a picture of your family as Anna does. Don't forget to add names of family members and to include yourself in your drawing. Tell about your drawing to introduce your family to your classmates.

Tell What You Hear As Anna's class finds out, everyone hears something different as they listen to music. Bring in some music without words. Ask classmates to tell what they hear.

Make a Collage Find pictures in old magazines of favorite foods, sports, or anything that gives a hint about who you are and what you like. Paste the pictures in a design on paper. Display your collage with collages your classmates made. Guess who made each one.

More Books About Challenges

Herbie Jones by Suzy Kline
Herbie is tired of being in the Apples reading group, but his best friend, Raymond, is in the Apples with him. Can Herbie leave Raymond?

Fidelia by Ruth Adams
Coming from a musical family, it's only natural that Fidelia would want to make music. She's too young to play the violin, but with her older brother's help, she creates an instrument that surprises everyone.

Wesley Paul, Marathon Runner
by Julianna A. Fogel
Wesley Paul comes home after school, changes clothes, and has a snack just as you might do. Then, rain or shine, he runs at least ten miles each day to prepare for long-distance races. It's exciting, but it's hard work too!

Thinking Big by Susan Kuklin
Jaime Osborn will never grow to be full size. Sometimes when Jaime goes out, people stare at her. Find out how Jaime meets special challenges every day of her life.

Written and Illustrated
by Dr. Seuss

The SNEETCHES

The SNEETCHES

The Plain-Belly Sneetches aren't having any fun these days. The Star-Belly Sneetches are leaving them out of *everything*. Belonging to a group you like can be lots of fun. But being left out is no fun at all.

For the Fun of Reading Dr. Seuss

Maybe you've read some of Dr. Seuss's books. He makes up silly characters like Sneetches. Sneetches are not exactly animals or people but something in between. Even though Dr. Seuss's creatures don't look like people, they can have the same feelings people have. In *The Sneetches,* one group of creatures learns what it feels like to be left out by another group of Sneetches just because they don't wear stars.

Dr. Seuss tells his story of the Sneetches in a story poem. To make his poem rhyme, he sometimes makes up his own words. Dr. Seuss uses the word "thars" to rhyme with "stars," and "eaches" to rhyme with "beaches." In his funny story, Dr. Seuss shows you something about the feelings and problems that Sneetches, and people, may have.

The Sneetches' Troubles

Dr. Seuss's *The Sneetches* tells a story about some trouble between two groups of characters, the Star-Belly Sneetches and the Plain-Belly Sneetches. The trouble that the Star-Belly Sneetches cause and how the Sneetches solve their problems make up the action in the story.

As you're reading the story poem on your own, find out how the Sneetches' troubles finally end.

The SNEETCHES

Now, the Star-Belly Sneetches
Had bellies with stars.
The Plain-Belly Sneetches
Had none upon thars.

Those stars weren't so big. They were really so small
You might think such a thing wouldn't matter at all.

But, because they had stars, all the Star-Belly Sneetches
Would brag, "We're the best kind of Sneetch on the beaches."
With their snoots in the air, they would sniff and they'd snort
"We'll have nothing to do with the Plain-Belly sort!"
And whenever they met some, when they were out walking,
They'd hike right on past them without even talking.

When the Star-Belly children went out to play ball,
Could a Plain Belly get in the game . . . ? Not at all.
You only could play if your bellies had stars
And the Plain-Belly children had none upon thars.

When the Star-Belly Sneetches had frankfurter roasts
Or picnics or parties or marshmallow toasts,
They never invited the Plain-Belly Sneetches.
They left them out cold, in the dark of the beaches.
They kept them away. Never let them come near.
And that's how they treated them year after year.

Then ONE day, it seems . . . while the Plain-Belly Sneetches
Were moping and doping alone on the beaches,
Just sitting there wishing their bellies had stars . . .
A stranger zipped up in the strangest of cars!

"My friends," he announced in a voice clear and keen,
"My name is Sylvester McMonkey McBean.
 And I've heard of your troubles. I've heard you're unhappy.
 But I can fix that. I'm the Fix-it-Up Chappie.
 I've come here to help you. I have what you need.
 And my prices are low. And I work at great speed.
 And my work is one hundred per cent guaranteed!"

Then, quickly, Sylvester McMonkey McBean
Put together a very peculiar machine.
And he said, "You want stars like a Star-Belly Sneetch . . . ?
My friends, you can have them for three dollars each!"

"Just pay me your money and hop right aboard!"
So they clambered inside. Then the big machine roared
And it klonked. And it bonked. And it jerked. And it berked
And it bopped them about. But the thing really worked!
When the Plain-Belly Sneetches popped out, they had stars!
They actually did. They had stars upon thars!

Then they yelled at the ones who had stars at the start,
"We're exactly like you! You can't tell us apart.
We're all just the same, now, you snooty old smarties!
And now we can go to your frankfurter parties."

"Good grief!" groaned the ones who had stars at the first.
"We're *still* the best Sneetches and they are the worst.
But, now, how in the world will we know," they all frowned,
"If which kind is what, or the other way round?"

Then up came McBean with a very sly wink
And he said, "Things are not quite as bad as you think.
So you don't know who's who. That is perfectly true.
But come with me, friends. Do you know what I'll do?
I'll make you, again, the best Sneetches on beaches
And all it will cost you is ten dollars eaches."

"Belly stars are no longer in style," said McBean.
"What you need is a trip through my Star-*Off* Machine.
This wondrous contraption will take *off* your stars
So you won't look like Sneetches who have them on thars."
And that handy machine
Working very precisely
Removed all the stars from their tummies quite nicely.

Then, with snoots in the air, they paraded about
And they opened their beaks and they let out a shout,
"We know who is who! Now there isn't a doubt.
The best kind of Sneetches are Sneetches without!"

Then, of course, those with stars all got frightfully mad.
To be wearing a star now was frightfully bad.
Then, of course, old Sylvester McMonkey McBean
Invited *them* into his Star-Off Machine.

Then, of course from THEN on, as you probably guess,
Things really got into a horrible mess.

All the rest of that day, on those wild screaming beaches,
The Fix-it-Up Chappie kept fixing up Sneetches.
Off again! On again!
In again! Out again!
Through the machines they raced round and about again,
Changing their stars every minute or two.
They kept paying money. They kept running through
Until neither the Plain nor the Star-Bellies knew
Whether this one was that one . . . or that one was this one
Or which one was what one . . . or what one was who.

Then, when every last cent
Of their money was spent,
The Fix-it-Up Chappie packed up
And he went.

And he laughed as he drove
In his car up the beach,
"They never will learn.
No. You can't teach a Sneetch!"

But McBean was quite wrong. I'm quite happy to say
That the Sneetches got really quite smart on that day,
The day they decided that Sneetches are Sneetches
And no kind of Sneetch is the best on the beaches.
That day, all the Sneetches forgot about stars
And whether they had one, or not, upon thars.

Responding to Literature

1. Sylvester McMonkey McBean and his machines help the Star-Belly and Plain-Belly Sneetches to become smarter. If you could, would you change any part of the story? Tell why or why not.

2. Pretend that you are a Sneetch and someone asks you what Sylvester McMonkey McBean's machines can do. What would you tell that person?

3. The Star-Belly and Plain-Belly Sneetches solve their problems in an unusual way. How do the Sneetches' troubles finally end?

4. You can read a Dr. Seuss story to find out what it's all about or just for the fun of it. Was reading *The Sneetches* fun for you? Explain your answer.

The WOZZIT

There's a wozzit in the closet
and it's making quite a mess.
It has eaten father's trousers,
it has eaten mother's dress,
and it's making so much noise
as it gobbles down my toys,
there's a wozzit in the closet—
oh I'm certain . . . yes, oh yes!

There's a wozzit in the closet
and I don't know what to do.
It has swallowed sister's slippers,
it has chewed upon my shoe,
now it's having its dessert
for it's stuffing down my shirt,
there's a wozzit in the closet—
yes, oh yes, I know it's true!

And I also know I'll never never
open up that closet,
for I never never never
ever
want to meet that wozzit.

Jack Prelutsky

Finding Out About the Story

Thinking About Conflict

In *The Sneetches*, Dr. Seuss chose to write a story about the trouble between two groups of characters, the Star-Belly Sneetches and the Plain-Belly Sneetches. Just because the Star-Bellies "have stars upon thars," Dr. Seuss writes how poorly they treat the Plain-Bellies.

"They kept them away. Never let them come near.
And that's how they treated them year after year."

Dr. Seuss creates characters who don't get along. He does this so that you will be interested in them and want to see how they solve their problems, especially when the solution is as silly as McBean's funny machines.

Writing About Conflict

Suppose that instead of McBean, *you* came to help the Sneetches. What silly solution would you suggest?

Prewriting Imagine that the Sneetches ask for solutions to put in a suggestion box. Write on a card the funny idea that McBean has for solving the Sneetches' problems. Then write your own funny idea on another card. (For ideas about writing, turn to the Handbook.)

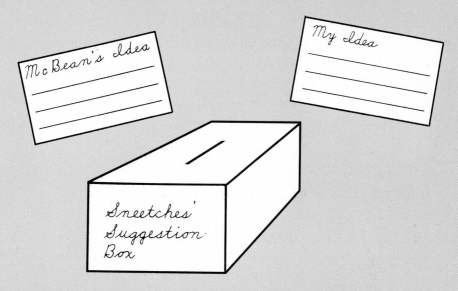

Writing Write a paragraph to persuade the Sneetches to use your idea for solving their problems. Convince the Sneetches that you have a great idea. Use your best reason at the end of your paragraph. That will convince the Sneetches that you can do the job.

Revising Exchange your draft with a partner. Listen as your partner reads your draft aloud. Does your idea sound convincing? Do you think your idea will appeal to the Sneetches? If not, revise your draft. Make changes to make your paragraph more convincing.

Presenting Draw a big picture or make a large chart to show how your idea works. Then present your idea to a group of classmates who pretend to be Sneetches.

Extending Your Reading

Expressing Yourself
Choose one or more of these activities:

Create a Character Using cardboard, styrofoam cups, sticks, and scraps of fabric, make new kinds of creatures who are as silly as the Sneetches. Think of funny names for your creatures. Make up a story about them.

Direct a TV Movie Direct a TV version of *The Sneetches*. Choose classmates to read parts of the story while other classmates act it out. Make stars, McBean's machines, and other things you need for your movie from paper or cardboard.

Make a "McBean Wanted" Ad Pretend you are a Sneetch. Prepare a radio announcement warning other Sneetches or people about Sylvester McMonkey McBean. Present your announcement to your class and tell how he looks. Warn everybody about what he might try to do.

Read More Dr. Seuss Books At the library, find a Dr. Seuss book to read to the class or to place in a "Dr. Seuss library" along with other Dr. Seuss books your classmates have found. Discuss with a partner which book is your favorite.

More Humorous Books

The Queen and Rosie Randall by Helen Oxenbury
The King of Wottermazzy is coming. The Queen
is at her wit's end trying to decide how to entertain
him. She calls on Rosie Randall for advice, and
Rosie plans a never-to-be-forgotten royal party.

What's So Funny, Ketu? by Verna Aardema
Ketu can't tell anybody what he thinks is so
funny. For saving the life of a snake, Ketu gains
the power to hear the thoughts of animals. Who
would have guessed that animals have such
funny thoughts?

The Princess and the Pumpkin by Maggie Duff
The Princess keeps growing weaker and weaker.
Someone must make her laugh. Everyone tries
their funniest jokes, songs, and tricks but the
Princess won't even smile. Then Granny comes
to town. She knows she can help.

Chester the Worldly Pig by Bill Peet
Chester already knows what he would amount
to in life—bacon, ham, or sausage. He intends
to try to change his future. A circus poster gives
him a spectacular idea.

CRINKLEROOT

HATBAND

WALKING STICK —

MOCCASINS

🐾 CRINKLEROOT WAS BORN IN A TREE AND RAISED BY BEES.

🐾 HE CAN WHISTLE IN A HUNDRED LANGUAGES AND SPEAK CATERPILLAR, SALAMANDER, AND TURTLE.

🐾 HE KNOWS ALL ABOUT WILD ANIMALS, EVEN THE ONES THAT LIVE AROUND YOUR HOUSE!

🐾 CRINKLEROOT LIVES IN THE DEEP WOODS AND HIS FAVORITE FOOD IS POPCORN.

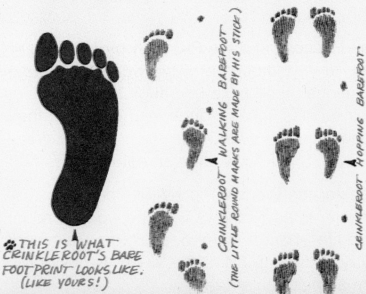

🐾 THIS IS WHAT CRINKLEROOT'S BARE FOOT PRINT LOOKS LIKE. (LIKE YOURS!)

CRINKLEROOT WALKING BAREFOOT (THE LITTLE ROUND MARKS ARE MADE BY HIS STICK)

CRINKLEROOT HOPPING BAREFOOT

Crinkleroot's

BOOK OF

ANIMAL TRACKS
AND
WILDLIFE SIGNS

Written and Illustrated by

Jim Arnosky

Crinkleroot's
BOOK OF
ANiMAL TRACKS
AND
WiLDLiFE SiGNS

Have you ever wanted to be a detective, hunt for clues, and solve mysteries? You can become a nature detective and use clues such as animal tracks to solve wildlife mysteries. If you want to know more about animals, a character named Crinkleroot can help. Crinkleroot loves to solve wildlife mysteries.

Meet a Nature Detective

Crinkleroot is a make-believe character who is interested in nature and in studying animals in the wild. Just like Crinkleroot, you can study nature too. You can look for wildlife near where you live by noticing tracks and wildlife signs that show animals are there. Using tracks as a clue, you can figure out what kind of animal is near. Crinkleroot shows you how it's done.

If Crinkleroot sees tracks near a pond, he knows they could belong to a raccoon, an otter, or a beaver.

DEER

WEASEL

RACCOON

Crinkleroot tells you about the animals that make the woods their home. He shows you signs that let you know that a deer or owl may be hiding among the trees. Learning how Crinkleroot solves animal mysteries near water and in the woods can help you solve animal mysteries wherever you are.

How the Author Writes About Animals

Jim Arnosky, the author of *Crinkleroot's Book of Animal Tracks and Wildlife Signs,* shares facts about animals in his own interesting way. He chooses to use drawings and charts, and has an imaginary character named Crinkleroot lead you near water and through the woods.

As you're reading the article on your own, find out how animal tracks and signs can help you find animals.

Crinkleroot's
BOOK OF
ANIMAL TRACKS
AND
WILDLIFE SIGNS

Hello. You've been following Crinkleroot tracks. My name is Crinkleroot, and these are my tracks.

I can hear a fox turn in the forest and spot a mole hole on a mountain. I can find an owl in the daytime.

Animals are everywhere. They live in forests and towns and even in cities. The marks and tracks they leave behind are called their signs. When you've lived in the woods as long as I have, you learn to read these signs. They show where the animals have been and what they've been doing. When I walk about the forest, I leave signs that tell I've been around—my footprints.

I can show you how I find signs of animals that live near me. Then you can look for signs of animals that live near you.

TRACKS AND WILDLIFE SIGNS AROUND WATER 🐾

One of the best places to look for wildlife signs is around water. Animals are attracted to streams and ponds, to park fountains, and even to damp patches of grass. That's because they find water to drink there and food to hunt.

This pond was built by beavers. Can you see what shows me that this is a beaver pond?

Beavers build a pond by blocking up a stream with branches, sticks, and mud. Their construction is called a beaver dam. Finding a dam like this is a sure sign that beavers are living in a pond.

Beavers are large rodents. All rodents have sharp gnawing teeth, but a beaver is the only rodent that can gnaw down a tree! After a beaver fells a tree, he pulls it into the water. When a tree is too heavy to move, the beaver chews it into small logs and rolls each one into the pond. The beaver then pushes the floating log to wherever it's needed.

Sometimes a beaver gets lucky, and the tree falls right into the pond!

Beavers use logs and chewed-off pieces of trees to build their dams and their homes, or lodges.

Beavers also eat the wood from the trees they chop down. They eat the bark first. Then they gnaw off the small branches and store them on the bottom of the pond. In winter, when the pond is frozen over, they will use the branches for food. Chewed-down trees and gnawed-off twigs are good beaver signs to look for.

407

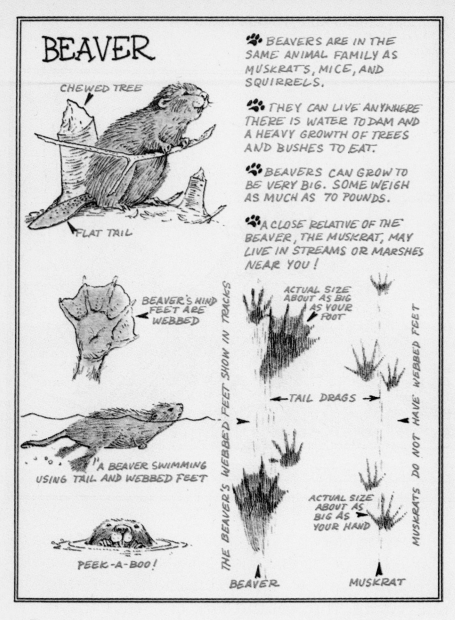

BEAVER

- CHEWED TREE
- FLAT TAIL

🐾 BEAVERS ARE IN THE SAME ANIMAL FAMILY AS MUSKRATS, MICE, AND SQUIRRELS.

🐾 THEY CAN LIVE ANYWHERE THERE IS WATER TO DAM AND A HEAVY GROWTH OF TREES AND BUSHES TO EAT.

🐾 BEAVERS CAN GROW TO BE VERY BIG. SOME WEIGH AS MUCH AS 70 POUNDS.

🐾 A CLOSE RELATIVE OF THE BEAVER, THE MUSKRAT, MAY LIVE IN STREAMS OR MARSHES NEAR YOU!

BEAVER'S HIND FEET ARE WEBBED

THE BEAVER'S WEBBED FEET SHOW IN TRACKS

ACTUAL SIZE ABOUT AS BIG AS YOUR FOOT

← TAIL DRAGS →

"A BEAVER SWIMMING USING TAIL AND WEBBED FEET

ACTUAL SIZE ABOUT AS BIG AS YOUR HAND

MUSKRATS DO NOT HAVE WEBBED FEET

PEEK-A-BOO!

BEAVER   MUSKRAT

Beavers have webbed feet for swimming and flat tails for steering through water. Both show their tracks.

Let's wade around the shallow edges of the pond and look for other wildlife signs.

Here are more webbed footprints, but these aren't beaver tracks. These tracks were made by an otter. Otters are large water weasels. They are the only weasels that have webbed feet. They eat fish, frogs, snakes, and turtles. Full-grown otters will even eat baby beavers.

Most of an otter's life is spent in the quiet underwater world of a pond. An otter can outswim a trout!

Otters are carefree critters. Entire families of otters play for hours, sliding down muddy spots on the pond bank and splashing into the water.

"Otter slides" are smooth and slippery from wet otters sliding down them again and again. You may have seen otters sliding at the zoo.

OTTER

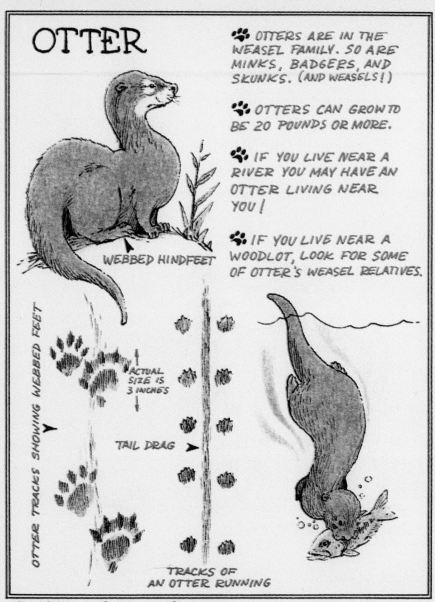

🐾 OTTERS ARE IN THE WEASEL FAMILY. SO ARE MINKS, BADGERS, AND SKUNKS. (AND WEASELS!)

🐾 OTTERS CAN GROW TO BE 20 POUNDS OR MORE.

🐾 IF YOU LIVE NEAR A RIVER YOU MAY HAVE AN OTTER LIVING NEAR YOU!

🐾 IF YOU LIVE NEAR A WOODLOT, LOOK FOR SOME OF OTTER'S WEASEL RELATIVES.

WEBBED HINDFEET

OTTER TRACKS SHOWING WEBBED FEET

ACTUAL SIZE IS 3 INCHES

TAIL DRAG

TRACKS OF AN OTTER RUNNING

OTTERS ARE THE ONLY WEASELS MORE AT HOME IN WATER THAN ON LAND.

Otters rarely build a house, or den, of their own. Usually they move into dens that other water animals such as muskrats and beavers have moved out of. Otters like two entrances—one on land and one underwater. If the den they move into has only one entrance, they dig out a second one.

410

These footprints belong to an animal that feels at home wherever there's water nearby. These tracks were made by a raccoon family. A raccoon's footprints look like the prints of tiny human hands and feet.

Raccoons live in forests, parks, towns, and cities. They build their dens in hollow trees, rocky ledges, even in sewer pipes and drain pipes. If you find raccoon tracks, they might lead you right to a den. Look for signs of raccoons near your home.

Raccoons eat almost anything they can catch or find. They even raid garbage cans. Raccoons come to the pond to hunt for crayfish, frogs, snails, and freshwater clams.

Like many wild animals, raccoons are nocturnal—that means they are more active at night than during the day. One night I watched a

RACCOON

- A RACCOON CAN BE BROWN OR GRAY WITH A MASK OF BLACK FUR ON IT'S FACE AND BLACK RINGS ON IT'S TAIL.

- MOST RACCOONS WEIGH BETWEEN 10 POUNDS AND 15 POUNDS.

- RACCOONS GRUNT, GROWL, HISS, AND SOMETIMES THEY CHUCKLE.

- A RACCOON'S TEETH ARE AS BIG AS A DOG'S TEETH — ONLY MUCH SHARPER.

RAIDING A CORNFIELD

RACCOON'S FRONT FOOT

ACTUAL SIZE 2 INCHES

RACCOON'S HIND FOOT

ACTUAL SIZE 4 INCHES

A RACCOON WALKING

RACCOONS ARE EXPERT CLIMBERS

— AND SWIMMERS.

SUNNING ON A LIMB

raccoon reach under the rocks in the shallow water of the pond. It was feeling for a crayfish hiding there. The raccoon had a bushy, ringed tail and a black patch of fur across its bright eyes. It looked like a bandit in the moonlight.

Here are lots of raccoon tracks in the mud. Follow them and see what they tell you. What did the big raccoons catch and eat? How many baby raccoons were there?

TRACKS AND WILDLIFE SIGNS IN THE WOODS ❖❖

A patch of woods is a good place to look for wildlife signs. Many of the shyest creatures live in the woods. They hide among the trees and shadows. They eat twigs, buds, nuts, and seeds.

Deer are large, hooved animals that live in forests and in woodlots outside of towns and cities. They tramp trails all through the woods, searching for food and water. Look for the heart-shaped tracks of their hooves in the mush of trampled leaves and soil.

Every summer the male deer, which are called bucks, grow a set of antlers on their heads. During the time they are growing, the antlers are covered with a layer of fuzzy skin called velvet. The velvet is filled with blood vessels that make the antlers grow quickly.

In autumn, when the antlers are fully grown, the fuzzy skin begins to dry up and peel. The bucks scrape it off by rubbing their antlers against the bark of small trees and bushes. This causes worn, smooth spots on the trees, which are called buck rubs. Buck rubs are a sure sign that a buck has been using a trail.

Rubbing also sharpens the antlers' points. A healthy buck may have many points on his antlers. He is ready for any fight. Bucks fight each other to see who will mate with the female deer, which are called does.

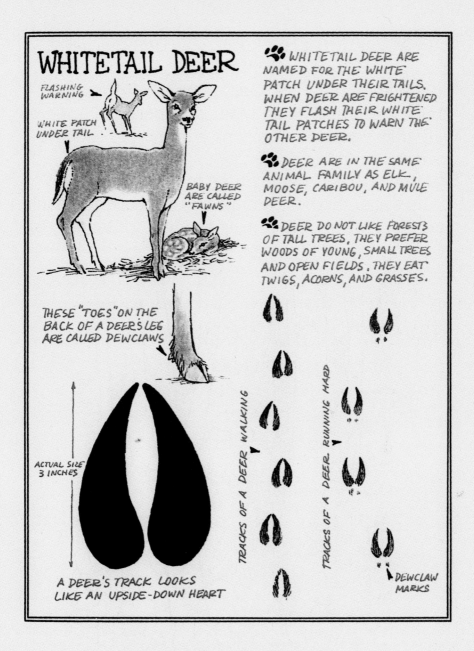

WHITETAIL DEER

FLASHING WARNING

WHITE PATCH UNDER TAIL

BABY DEER ARE CALLED "FAWNS"

🐾 WHITETAIL DEER ARE NAMED FOR THE WHITE PATCH UNDER THEIR TAILS. WHEN DEER ARE FRIGHTENED THEY FLASH THEIR WHITE TAIL PATCHES TO WARN THE OTHER DEER.

🐾 DEER ARE IN THE SAME ANIMAL FAMILY AS ELK, MOOSE, CARIBOU, AND MULE DEER.

🐾 DEER DO NOT LIKE FORESTS OF TALL TREES, THEY PREFER WOODS OF YOUNG, SMALL TREES AND OPEN FIELDS, THEY EAT TWIGS, ACORNS, AND GRASSES.

THESE "TOES" ON THE BACK OF A DEER'S LEG ARE CALLED DEWCLAWS

ACTUAL SIZE 3 INCHES

A DEER'S TRACK LOOKS LIKE AN UPSIDE-DOWN HEART

TRACKS OF A DEER WALKING

TRACKS OF A DEER RUNNING HARD

DEWCLAW MARKS

In winter, when the fuzzy, nourishing layer of skin is gone and the mating season is over, a buck's antlers fall off. Each buck is left with two small, smooth spots on his head where the antlers will grow again the following summer, in time for next fall's mating season.

Antlers that have fallen off are eaten by mice, squirrels, and other hungry forest nibblers. A buck has shed his antlers in this patch of winter woods.

Can you find them? Sometimes antlers fall off one at a time, so you might not find a set together.

Owls are nocturnal. But I can find owls in the daytime. So can you.

Owls are birds of prey. They live where there are mice and rats to catch. When an owl eats a mouse, it swallows it whole—tail and all. The owl's stomach digests everything except the mouse's bones and fur. The bones and fur form a ball which the owl coughs up and out onto the ground.

OWL PELLET
ACTUAL SIZE

These balls of bones and fur are called owl pellets. They collect on the ground around trees where owls have been roosting. You can look for these pellets around the trees near your home. If you find some, look in the tree above for an owl sleeping the day away. That's how I find owls in the daytime.

I've seen a lot of tracks here in the forest. I've even tracked fleas through the fur on a bear's back. But I can't seem to recognize these tracks next to my own.

Why, they must be yours.

The next time you go for a walk, look for animal marks and tracks. Look for signs of stray cats in your neighborhood, and follow your dog's tracks to see if it's been up to mischief!

Wherever you live there are animals living near you. Study my charts and look for the signs animals leave in parks and woodlots, on pavements and sidewalks, under trees, around streams and ponds, and in the snow. I can't promise you'll find any flea tracks, but you'll find something. And if you hear a soft swish in the night, go back to sleep. It's just a fox turning around somewhere in the forest.

Meet the Author and Illustrator: **Jim Arnosky**

Jim Arnosky wrote *Crinkleroot's Book of Animal Tracks and Wildlife Signs* to tell about the animals who live near his home. Mr. Arnosky enjoys nature and wildlife, and he hopes that his character Crinkleroot will make his readers as excited about tracking and observing wild animals as he is. He describes Crinkleroot as a "woodsman who knows endless wonders about the natural world and teaches them to his readers through activities they can join in."

If you would like to learn more about nature and wildlife, you might want to read *A Kettle of Hawks and Other Wildlife Groups* by Jim Arnosky.

Responding to Literature

1. Crinkleroot tells you many facts about wild animals and their signs. Which fact is most interesting to you? Why?

2. Pretend you are leading a group on a trip to a pond. Suppose someone spots a beaver pond and asks you how the beaver built its home. What would you say?

3. Of all the animals that Crinkleroot tells you about, which three animals would you most like to watch in the wild? Tell how tracks or signs could help you find these three different animals.

4. A mystery can be something that is hidden. How is looking for signs of wildlife like solving a mystery?

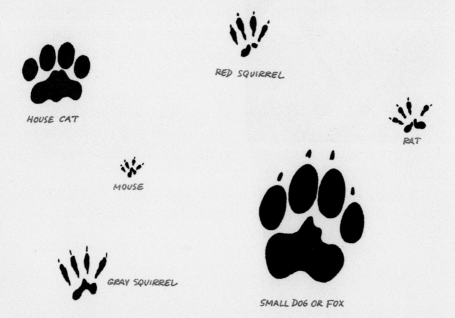

RED SQUIRREL

HOUSE CAT

RAT

MOUSE

GRAY SQUIRREL

SMALL DOG OR FOX

Los Sapos

Trozos de barro,
por la senda en penumbra
saltan los sapos.

José Juan Tablada

The Toads

Chunks of mud,
the toads hop
down the unlighted path.

Translated by Hardie St. Martin

Finding Out About the Article ✿

Thinking About the Author's Style

In writing *Crinkleroot's Book of Animal Facts and Wildlife Signs,* author Jim Arnosky writes about wild animals in a way that's fun to read. Instead of just telling you facts about animals, he chooses to use a make-believe character named Crinkleroot to guide you on a nature walk. The author has Crinkleroot tell you facts in this way.

> "Otters are carefree critters. Entire families of otters play for hours, sliding down muddy spots on the pond bank and splashing into the water."

Using Crinkleroot as your guide, and using his charts and drawings, the author helps you have fun finding out about wildlife.

Writing in Your Own Style

How would you choose to tell facts about a wild animal? Write a report in your own way.

Prewriting On your own paper, make a chart like the one on the next page. Fill in information about raccoons from the article. Choose a wild animal to add to your chart. Look up facts about that animal to fill in your chart. (For ideas about writing, turn to the Handbook.)

SKUNK

MUSKRAT

OPOSSUM

	Food	Tracks	Other Clues
Raccoons			

Writing Write a report that tells the facts you learned about the animal you chose, and how to recognize that animal in the wild. Think of an interesting way that you can tell the facts. Use drawings of your animal and diagrams of its tracks to make your report fun to read and easy to understand.

Revising Exchange your draft with a partner. Listen as your partner reads it aloud. Does your report tell interesting facts about your animal? Does your report tell how to recognize it? If not, revise your draft so that it tells facts about your animal and tells how to recognize it. Write your final copy.

Presenting Pretend you are Crinkleroot. Give a nature talk about the animal in your report. Share your drawings with your classmates.

WOODCHUCK

CHIPMUNK

COTTONTAIL RABBIT

Extending Your Reading

Expressing Yourself
Choose one or more of these activities:

Be an Animal Detective With a partner, take a wildlife walk around your schoolyard or home. Look for animal signs and try to figure out which animals left the signs and why. Then share your findings with a small group of classmates.

Build a Model Construct a model of a beaver dam and lodge. Use Crinkleroot's diagram to show you how it should look. Instead of using trees, branches, and mud as a beaver would, use small twigs or toothpicks and clay.

Make a Guide Book Make a picture guide book of wildlife in your neighborhood. Make color pictures to show how the animal looks. Include the animal's name, what the animal's tracks look like, its size, and interesting habits.

Choose a Mystery Animal What's black and white and makes its own perfume? Give a few clues about an animal and have classmates guess what it is. See how many of your classmates' mystery animals you can recognize.

SMALL OWL

DUCK

More Books About Nature

A Penguin Year by Susan Bonners
Find out how penguins can live in one of the coldest places on earth. Once a year, millions of penguins swim the freezing sea and march across ice to reach their nesting place in the South Pole. Join these birds by reading about their journey.

Strange Animals of Australia by Toni Eugene
Australia seems to have more than its share of unusual animals. Even their names may sound strange to you. Meet the numbat, the wombat, the bandicoot, and the platypus.

Where the Waves Break: Life at the Edge of the Sea by Anita Malnig
If you have ever seen an ocean, you know how big and exciting it is. This book will show you the smaller, quieter parts of oceans around the world. You'll find out about starfish, sand dollars, and other animals who live in the oceans' tide pools and shallow waters.

A Forest Is Reborn by James R. Newton
A fire destroys a beautiful old forest. All that remain are blackened tree trunks and a burned forest floor. It doesn't seem possible, but a forest can grow again. Find out how it happens.

SPARROW
(A HOPPER)

PIGEON
(A WALKER)

Clancy's Coat

by Eve Bunting

Illustrated by
Lorinda Bryan Cauley

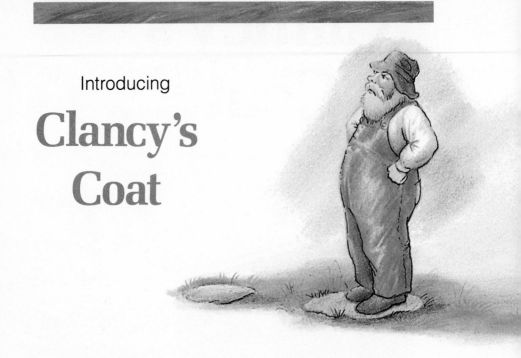

Introducing

Clancy's Coat

Have you ever had a quarrel with your best friend? Did you feel grumpy and angry, and think you'd never want to see that awful person again? That's the way Tippitt and Clancy feel in *Clancy's Coat.* Will they ever be friends again?

Neighbors and Friends

In a country glen in Ireland, two neighbors, Tippitt and Clancy, know what it's like to live far from the nearest town. As neighbors, they often count on each other. Tippitt is glad for the vegetables Clancy shares from his garden. Clancy knows Tippitt is the best tailor around for fixing his clothes. As friends, Tippitt and Clancy enjoy visiting with each other. Why, then, would the two friends quarrel?

Characters Who Change

Eve Bunting, the author of *Clancy's Coat,* chose to write a story about a quarrel between two friends. She shows you how the characters Tippitt and Clancy feel about each other by what they say and do. The author shows you how the characters feel about each other at the beginning of the story and how their feelings change by the end.

As you're reading on your own, find out why Tippitt and Clancy change their feelings.

Clancy's Coat

T ippitt the tailor was having his morning tea when he looked out the window and saw Clancy coming along the road.

"Well, I'll be jakered," he said to Sam, his sheepdog. Hadn't old Clancy sworn never to look in Tippitt's direction again? Hadn't he insulted Tippitt, and Tippitt's good cow, Bridget, too, just because Bridget forgot her manners one day and got into Clancy's vegetable garden?

"Here comes trouble, Sam," Tippitt said, shading his eyes from the sun. "We'll wait for it at the door, for there's no sense inviting trouble into your house."

It wasn't till Clancy got closer that Tippitt saw he was carrying a parcel.

"I've brought you work to do," Clancy said, stopping in front of them. "And I've brought it for the reason that you're the best tailor in Crossgar, and not for the sake of old friendships. Though we were the best of friends and the best of neighbors once, in the days before your cow destroyed my garden."

Tippitt stepped aside and so did Sam. "If it's work you need done you'd better come in."

"I'll come in, then, but I'll not be staying."

"And who asked you to stay?" Tippitt pushed away the teapot and made room on the table for the parcel.

Clancy undid the string and pulled out an old, black coat, shiny with time and wear. Sam cringed back from the smell of mothballs.

"There's a lot of use left in this old coat," Clancy said. "It was a fine piece of cloth and it just needs turning." He pulled one of the sleeves out to show the red wool lining.

"What I need is for you to make the inside be the outside and the outside be the inside, if you get my meaning."

Tippitt raised his eyebrows. "Surely. The coat needs turning."

"That's it." Clancy hung it on the back of a chair and rubbed his hands together. "Powerful cold out." He eyed the brown teapot with the steam rising from its spout.

Tippitt made no move to take another mug from the dresser. "You said you wouldn't be staying."

"Right," Clancy said. "When will the coat be ready?"

"By Saturday."

"I'll be here for it."

Tippitt and Sam watched Clancy go. "It was a sorry day when Bridget got in his vegetables," Tippitt said. "He's a great man for his growing things. It comes from having neither chick nor child to call his own."

Sam nodded, the way he always did when Tippitt talked to him.

"Though my own children's grown and my wife is gone I still have you, my good cow, and my wee hen. All he has are his cabbages and turnips. It's not much, when all's said and done."

Sam nodded again and Tippitt examined the coat. "It'll be as easy to do as skimming cream," he said. "And it'll be done for Saturday."

It would have been, too, except that the night was extra cold, and in the middle of it Tippitt heard Bridget mooing in the barn. When he got up and looked for something to put round her to keep her warm, there was Clancy's coat. Tippitt took it out, spread it over the cow, and forgot all about it till the next Saturday when he was having dinner and looked out to see Clancy heading up the road.

436

"Jakers!" Tippitt said to Sam. "Didn't I forget all about Clancy's coat! We'd better invite him to stay a while this time, for he'll be powerful annoyed and in need of soothing."

"Come in, come in," he called from the open door as Sam nodded and wagged his tail.

Clancy took off his muffler and set it on the dresser.

"I see you're eating your dinner," he said. "I'll not keep you, for I only came for my old coat."

"It's not ready yet," Tippitt said. "It's been over my . . . over . . . overlooked. But . . . ."

"Moo . . . oooo!" Bridget called from the barn.

"I'll have it for you for certain sure by next Saturday," Tippitt said quickly. "Would you have a cup of tea before you go?" He poured it from the pot, thick as tar and black as night.

"You always did make a good cup of tea." Clancy sat down at the table and eyed the remains of Tippitt's dinner. "Watery looking potatoes you have there. I'm thinking you bought those from O'Donnell of the Glen?"

"Aye," Tippitt said. "And they're like candle grease."

Clancy finished his tea and stood up. "I'll be back for the coat on Saturday."

When he opened the door the March wind came in, cold as Jack Frost's breath. "I'll be glad of that old coat," Clancy said, winding his muffler tight round his neck. "There's a lot of use in it yet."

Sam and Tippitt watched till he got all the way to his own wee house down the road, and then Tippitt went to the barn and got the coat from where Bridget was lying on it. And a hard job she made of it, for she didn't want to give it up.

Tippitt shook the hairs from it and set it next to his sewing machine. "I'll start on you in the morning," he told it. And he would have.

Only, that night the wind came up with a terrible fierceness and it blew the whole back window out of Tippitt's house, waking him from a sound sleep. In his hurry to find something to keep out the cold Tippitt saw the coat. He tacked it up where the glass had been and forgot all about it.

The next Saturday Clancy knocked at the door.

"Jakers save us!" Tippitt told Sam. "And the coat's not ready yet! This will take some quick thinking."

He pulled the best chair close to the fire and plumped out the cushions, and he and Sam were both smiling as they met Clancy at the door.

"Come in, sit down," Tippitt invited. "The coat's not fixed yet. It's been in my . . . in my . . . in my mind since I saw you last. But it'll be done by next Saturday for certain sure."

Tippitt noticed that Clancy had a sack slung over his shoulder. "What's this?" he asked.

"Potatoes," Clancy said. "I have them going to waste and I can't stand to see anybody eating poison like the ones you were eating last week. Not even you, Tippitt."

"Well, I'm much obliged." Tippitt decided to ignore the last part of the speech. "Will you have a cup of tea and a piece of my fresh baked bread before you go?"

He sliced a piece, spread it with butter, and carried it to where Clancy had seated himself in the best chair with its plumped up cushions.

"You always did have the whitest bread and the sweetest butter," Clancy said. "I can't buy the likes of it anywhere."

"It's Bridget's good buttermilk that goes into the both of them," Tippitt told him, and wished he'd been quiet because mention of Bridget might remind Clancy and set him off on another uproar.

But Clancy only said: "It's the care you give her. It shows up in what she gives back. Same as me and my garden."

Jakers, Tippitt thought, here it comes. But no more came.

"Saturday, then," Clancy said as he was leaving and Tippitt and Sam both nodded.

As soon as he'd gone Tippitt got the coat from the back window and nailed a piece of wood in its place. He put the coat on top of his sewing machine. "Don't be going any place else," he scolded it. "I'm getting to you tomorrow."

And he would have. Except that the very next day he remembered that he'd promised Rosie O'Brien her skirt for the Friday dance, so he threw Clancy's coat into the corner till he had time to get at it, and Mary, his hen, came right in and set herself on it. And the first thing Tippitt heard was her clucking and panting and swishing her feathers to get herself comfortable before laying her eggs.

Tippitt scratched his head. "Jakers, Sam! It wouldn't be decent to move Mary, and her in the middle of her business. We'll just have to put Clancy off again and we'll have to be smart about it."

On Saturday Tippitt moved his old sofa so that it hid Mary and the coat. He wrapped a big square of yellow butter and set it and a fresh brown loaf in the middle of the table.

"Och, the coat's not finished yet, Clance," he said when Clancy arrived and before he could ask.

"But there's good work being done on it, I'll promise you that."

Then he pointed to the butter and the bread. "I've a couple of wee presents for you here."

"It's a long time since you called me 'Clance,'" Clancy said gruffly. He set another sack on the table. "Here's a cabbage for you, and a bundle of leeks and carrots." His eyes slid away from Tippitt's and Tippitt knew he was wishing he'd never said 'garden' the week before just as Tippitt had wished he'd never said 'cow.'

447

They had tea together, sitting one on each side of the table, the fire flickering and the wee room as warm as toast. Tippitt asked about Clancy's bad leg and Clancy enquired about Tippitt's niece, the one who was married to a policeman and living in America.

"It's almost like old times," Clancy said as he got up to leave. "And I'll be back next week for the coat, for there's a lot of use in it yet."

Mary rustled behind the sofa and went "Cluck, cluck."

"This time, by jakers, he'll have it," Tippitt
told Sam as soon as Clancy had gone. "Get a
move on there with your business, Mary."

When the chicks were hatched Tippitt gently
moved them and thanked Mary kindly for her
trouble. Then he carried the coat outside and
spread it to air on the hawthorne hedge.

But when he went to take it in he saw that a
pair of sparrows were building a nest right in
the middle of it.

Tippitt scratched his head. "Well, there's not
a soul with a drop of kindness that would
disturb a pair of lovebirds when they're
building their nest. Should we tell Clance
what's going on with his coat, or should we try
putting him off another time? I'll admit to
something, Sam. I like having Clance around
again. And I noticed the way his hands
touched those carrots and leeks he brought
over. He loves them, so he does. I should have
tried harder to know how he felt when poor
Bridget stepped all over his garden."

Sam nodded.

"You think I should tell him where the coat
is, then?"

Sam nodded again.

When Clancy came he brought a bunch of new rhubarb, pink and tender.

"Isn't that the loveliest thing?" Tippitt said. "And inside there's some of Bridget's good cream to go along with it, sweet as sugar and thick enough to walk on. Now . . . about your coat . . . ."

"It's finished?" Clancy asked, and Tippitt thought he looked somehow disappointed.

"Not so you'd notice," he replied. He took Clancy out and showed him the sparrow's nest.

"Aye, it's spring," Clancy said. "The hedge is in blossom and the birds are building. Let them be, Tippitt. Sure I've no need of the coat till winter, now, and you'll have it done by then."

450

"You're a reasonable man, Clance," Tippitt said, and Sam nodded—twice.

"Not all the time," Clancy said. "But a man learns. A garden comes back with care and attention. I thought maybe a friendship could too."

Tippitt smiled and put his arm around Clancy's shoulders. "You're right," he said. "Now wasn't it the luckiest thing, Clance, that your old coat needed turning?"

Clancy winked. "I told you there was a lot of use left in it."

Tippitt chuckled. "Well, I'll be jakered!"

Meet the Author: **Eve Bunting**

Eve Bunting thought of the idea for writing *Clancy's Coat* when a friend lent her a book about a tailor. Mrs. Bunting says the book reminded her of growing up in Ireland, where her own family took their clothes to a tailor. She explains, "What I remember is that the clothes we took to be mended were never fixed on time. We had to keep going back to check on them. I thought that idea could be funny, so I made it into a story."

What does Mrs. Bunting like best about *Clancy's Coat*? She explains, "I just love the friendship part of the story."

Eve Bunting has written over one hundred thirty books for children and has received awards for her writing. If you'd like to read more books by Mrs. Bunting, look for *The Man Who Could Call Down Owls*, *The Traveling Men of Ballycoo*, and *Jane Martin, Dog Detective*.

Responding to Literature

1. Some books are interesting enough to read more than once. Do you think *Clancy's Coat* would be fun to read again? Why or why not?

2. Imagine that Sam can talk. Pretend you are Sam and answer this question. What happened after Clancy brought his coat to be fixed?

3. Clancy and Tippitt learn about themselves as they grow and change. At the beginning of the story, Clancy and Tippitt are angry with each other. By the end, they are friends again. Why do their feelings change?

4. What does Tippitt really mean when he says these things about Clancy's coat?
"It's been overlooked."   page 438
"It's been in my mind."   page 441
"There's good work being done on it."
page 446

Friendship

I've discovered a way to stay friends forever—
There's really nothing to it.
I simply tell you what to do
And you do it!

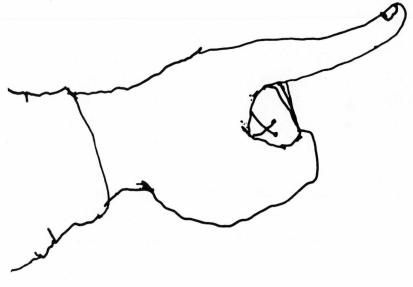

Shel Silverstein

Finding Out
About the Story

Thinking About Characters Who Change

In *Clancy's Coat,* Eve Bunting writes about two characters who change their feelings for each other. She shows how they feel at the beginning of the story and at the end. At first, Tippitt feels angry. When he sees Clancy, Tippitt says, "Here comes trouble." Clancy is angry too. He says, "We were the best of friends before your cow destroyed my garden."

Throughout the story, Mrs. Bunting gives you clues that the two may become friends again. Each time Clancy checks on his coat, he and Tippitt share food and time together. By the end, Tippitt and Clancy are good friends again.

Writing About Characters Who Change

Pretend you are a newspaper reporter for "The Glen News." You will write a story about Clancy and Tippitt.

Prewriting Think about what Clancy and Tippitt do for each other that helps them become friends again. Write two sentences that tell what either Clancy or Tippitt does for the other.

1. *Clancy gives Tippitt some rhubarb.*
2.
3.

Writing Write a news story about Clancy and Tippitt. Your job is to report *what* happened, and *where, when,* and *why* the two are friends again. Use ideas from your list to show what they did for each other. Give your story a headline that tells what it is about.

Revising Exchange your draft with a partner. Listen as your partner reads it aloud. Does your news story show why the friends changed? If not, revise your draft. Make changes so it shows a reason they are friends again. (For ideas about revising, turn to the Handbook.)

Presenting Draw a "photo" to go with your news story. Put your story and "photo" in a class newspaper for others to read.

Extending Your Reading

Expressing Yourself

Choose one or more of these activities:

Draw Clancy's Coat How do you think Clancy's coat might be used next? Draw a picture of the coat being used in a new way after the birds leave their nest.

Host a TV Interview Pretend you are on a TV show to tell how animals like living where they live. Choose three friends to be Sam, Mary, and Bridget. Use a "play" microphone, and ask how each animal feels about living with Tippitt. Be sure the three tell why they feel as they do.

Talk About What's Next With a group of classmates, discuss three questions. When will Clancy get his coat fixed? Do you think he will get it in time for next winter? Why or why not?

Act Out the Story Choose a part of the story to act out. With a partner, decide whether you will be Clancy or Tippitt. Wear a hat or glasses to show which character you are. Practice, read, and act out your part of the story for others.

More Books About Friends

Amos and Boris by William Steig
When Amos the rat rolls over and falls out of his homemade boat, the *Rodent,* he calls upon Boris the whale to rescue him. How could little Amos return the favor for his friend?

New Neighbors for Nora by Johanna Hurwitz
Nora, the oldest child in her neighborhood, is happy when new people move in. She's happy, that is, until she learns that the new kid on the block is one year older and a boy. They may be neighbors, but can they be friends?

The House at Pooh Corner by A. A. Milne
You're invited to Eeyore's house at Pooh Corner to meet Pooh, Piglet, Tigger, and Christopher Robin. In this book, you'll read about the funny adventures these friends share.

The Velveteen Rabbit by Margery Williams
Have you ever loved a stuffed animal so much that it seemed real to you? That happens to the boy in this story. If toys could talk, they might tell a story as this rabbit does.

This handbook will help you write well in response to the literature you have been reading. It answers the kinds of questions that you might ask when you are doing your writing assignments for Finding Out About the Story in this book as well as when you are doing other writing assignments. It is divided into four parts: prewriting, writing, revising, and presenting. Each part tells about one step of the writing process. The handbook also explains these four types of writing: narrative, descriptive, explanatory, and persuasive/analytical.

Prewriting

1. I know the topic I'm going to write about, but how can I organize my ideas and narrow my topic?

One way is to use a chart, such as the one on page 90. Another way is to use a web, or cluster diagram. A cluster diagram shows at a glance how a topic and details are related. To make a cluster diagram, first write a topic and circle it. Then draw circles below your topic and draw lines to connect them to the topic. Last, list details related to the topic inside the circles.

Notice in the cluster diagram below that the topic is *City Sights in a Blizzard*. Branching out from the topic are details that tell more about the topic.

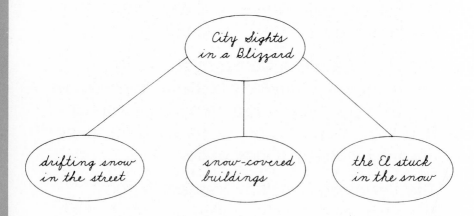

2. When I'm given a writing assignment, what is my first task?

When you receive a writing assignment, you should first decide on your *purpose* for writing and your *audience*. The people who will read your work are your *audience*. They may be your teacher, classmates, friends, family, or a writing partner. To determine your purpose, ask yourself: "What type of writing am I being asked to do?" Different types of writing have different purposes. Study the following chart to help you better understand your purpose for writing.

Type of writing	Purpose	Examples
narrative	• to tell a story about something that happened to a real or make-believe character • to tell the events in the order in which they happened	• dialogue • personal experience narrative • story ending • story
descriptive	• to paint a picture in words by using details that help the reader see, hear, feel, taste, or smell what you describe	• descriptive paragraph • journal entry • poem • post card
explanatory	• to tell how something is made or done • to tell the *who, what, where, why,* and *when*	• explanatory paragraph • news story
persuasive/ analytical	• to state your opinion and give reasons in order to convince others to share your opinion • to analyze facts and reach a conclusion	• persuasive paragraph • research report

461

1. Sometimes when I sit down, I just can't get started. What can I do then?

There are several ways to get started. Here are some suggestions.

Review Review what you did in Prewriting. Look for an idea that seems especially interesting.

Tune-Out Tuning out means letting go of all other distractions. For many people, this means no TV, radio, or phone calls. Set yourself up in a place where you can concentrate. Then take time to focus on your writing alone.

Push Ahead Sit down and pick up a pencil. Push your ideas out of your head and get them down on paper.

2. What is a first draft?

A first draft is like a trial run. First drafts give you a chance to get your ideas down. The writing and spelling does not have to be perfect. In fact, write a draft as freely as you can. Write whatever comes to mind on your subject. Don't stop writing and don't worry about perfect spelling, punctuation, or capitalization. If you stop to correct these kinds of errors, you may lose your train of thought.

1. I have just written my first draft. What do I do next?

Take a minute to read over your first draft. "Listen" to yourself. Think about your big point. Is it clear? Will it make sense to your audience? Also ask yourself if your writing achieves the purpose you set. Have you really written the type of writing you were assigned? Does your draft reflect the steps in that kind of writing?

The chart below tells what can make each type of writing good.

Type of Writing	What Makes It Good
narrative	• keeping to one main idea • telling events in time order • using signal words such as *first, next, then,* and *last* • including all the events that are important to the story
descriptive	• keeping to one main idea • choosing words that help the reader see, feel, hear, smell, or taste what you describe • being sure the sentences support the main idea • using colorful figures of speech
explanatory	• beginning with a topic sentence that tells what will be explained • following the topic sentence with details that support the main idea • telling the steps in order • making sure someone could follow the steps or understand the explanation • using examples to illustrate the steps
persuasive/ analytical	• keeping your audience in mind so you choose reasons and ideas that will appeal to them • beginning with a topic sentence that clearly states your opinion • using facts to support your opinion • drawing conclusions based on facts

2. What should I do when I revise?

First, revise your content. Have a writing conference with a small group, a partner, or your teacher. Read your draft aloud, and ask what is good and what could be better. Take notes on the comments. They will help you make changes.

3. How do I make changes?

There are four kinds of changes to make when you revise: adding, taking out, reordering, and proofreading. Each one is explained below.

<u>Adding Information</u> Reread your draft. Check to see if you left out any important information. For example, does your narrative paragraph have all the important events?

<u>Taking Out Unnecessary Information</u> Check to see that you have kept to your topic. Take out any sentences that don't belong. Also check for unnecessary words. Can you say the same thing in fewer words?

<u>Moving Words, Sentences, and Paragraphs</u> The order of your words, sentences, and paragraphs is what makes your writing clear. Have you told things in the right order? You may need to move some words or sentences.

<u>Proofreading</u> Finally, check your paper for mistakes in spelling, punctuation, capitalization, and form. Use the proofreading marks at the top of the next page to help you make these changes.

	Proofreader's Marks		
☰	Make a capital.	✐	Take out something.
⊙	Add a period.	⤳	Move something.
∧	Add something.	⟳sp	Correct spelling.

4. How can I be sure I've done a thorough job of revising?
You can use this Revision Checklist to check yourself.

Revision Checklist

Content
- ✔ Did I say what I wanted to say?
- ✔ Are my details in order?
- ✔ Does my composition have a beginning, a middle, and an end?
- ✔ Is each paragraph about one main idea? Does the topic sentence state that main idea?
- ✔ Are any of the pronouns confusing?
- ✔ Have I taken out the unnecessary words?

Mechanics
- ✔ Does each sentence begin with a capital letter?
- ✔ Does each sentence end with the correct punctuation mark?
- ✔ Are other punctuation marks used correctly—such as commas and quotation marks?
- ✔ Do subjects and verbs agree?
- ✔ Did I keep the correct verb tense throughout?
- ✔ Did I capitalize proper nouns and adjectives?
- ✔ Did I check the spelling of difficult words?
- ✔ Is my handwriting clear and neat?

1. What are some ways I can present my writing to others?
Here are some suggestions.

Read Aloud Read your paper to your classmates or family. Show expression in your voice. Then invite feedback. Ask questions such as, "Could you predict how my story would end?"

Make a Poster Paste your paper to a large piece of poster board. Draw a picture to illustrate it. Hang it on the bulletin board in your classroom.

Make a Book You can make a book that contains your best writing. To make a cover for your book, clip two pieces of heavy paper together. Then place a piece of three-holed notebook paper on top. Use a pencil to mark the holes and to punch them out. Write your book on notebook paper and then place the notebook paper between the covers. Push brass paper fasteners through the holes.

 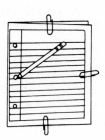 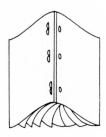

2. How can our class work together to present our writing?
Here are some ways your class can work together.

Start a Magazine Follow these steps:
a. As a class, think of a name for your magazine.
b. Ask for volunteers to copy the magazine.
c. Decide when and how often you will publish.
d. Choose a small group to be in charge of the magazine.
e. Along with your classmates, hand in the best examples of your writing. The magazine group will select what to include in each magazine issue.

Have a Puppet Show Follow these steps:
a. Rewrite one of your group stories as a play.
b. Help design and make a puppet for each part.
c. Put on the play, taking the part of the puppet you made.
d. Invite other classrooms to see your show.

Display Your Work for the School Ask your school principal if you and your classmates may display your work in the school lobby. Choose papers that are written about one specific topic. Help your group make a decorative border by drawing colorful pictures about the topic.

How to Use the Pronunciation Key

After each entry word in this glossary, there is a special spelling, called the **pronunciation.** It shows how to say the word. The word is broken into syllables and then spelled with letters and signs. You can look up these letters and signs in the **pronunciation key** to see what sounds they stand for.

This dark mark (′) is called the **primary accent.** It follows the syllable you say with the most force. This lighter mark (′) is the **secondary accent.** Say the syllable it follows with medium force. Syllables without marks are said with least force.

Full Pronunciation Key

a	hat, cap	i	it, pin	p	paper, cup	ə	stands for:
ā	age, face	ī	ice, five	r	run, try		a in about
ä	father, far			s	say, yes		e in taken
		j	jam, enjoy	sh	she, rush		i in pencil
b	bad, rob	k	kind, seek	t	tell, it		o in lemon
ch	child, much	l	land, coal	th	thin, both		u in circus
d	did, red	m	me, am	TH	then, smooth		
		n	no, in				
e	let, best	ng	long, bring	u	cup, butter		
ē	equal, be			u̇	full, put		
ėr	her, learn	o	hot, rock	ü	rule, move		
		ō	open, go				
f	fat, if	ô	order, all	v	very, save		
g	go, bag	oi	oil, toy	w	will, woman		
h	he, how	ou	house, out	y	young, yet		
				z	zoo, breeze		
				zh	measure, seizure		

The contents of the Glossary entries in this book have been adapted from *Scott, Foresman Beginning Dictionary*, Copyright © 1988 Scott, Foresman and Company; and *Scott, Foresman Intermediate Dictionary*, Copyright © 1988 Scott, Foresman and Company; and *Scott, Foresman Advanced Dictionary*, Copyright © 1988 Scott, Foresman and Company.

A

a·brupt (ə brupt′), **1** sudden: *The driver made an abrupt turn to avoid another car.* **2** short, sudden, and blunt: *She answered me with an abrupt remark and left.* *adjective.*
—**a·brupt′ly,** *adverb.*

ad·mit (ad mit′), say (something) is real or true; acknowledge: *I admit now that I made a mistake.* *verb,* **ad·mit·ted, ad·mit·ting.**

al·cove (al′kōv), a small room opening out of a larger room. *noun.*

al·tar (ôl′tər), table or stand used in religious worship in a church or temple: *The priest knelt in prayer before the altar. noun.*

altar—a Buddhist altar

an·noy (ə noi′), make somewhat angry; disturb: *The baby annoyed his sister by pulling her hair.* *verb.*

at·tract (ə trakt′), draw to itself or oneself: *The magnet attracted the iron filings.* *verb.*

au·di·tion (ô dish′ən), **1** a hearing to test the ability of a singer, actor, or other performer. **2** perform at or give such a hearing: *audition for a part in a play.* **1** *noun,* **2** *verb.*

a	hat	i	it	oi	oil	ch	child	ə	stands for:
ā	age	ī	ice	ou	out	ng	long		a in about
ä	far	o	hot	u	cup	sh	she		e in taken
e	let	ō	open	u̇	put	th	thin		i in pencil
ē	equal	ô	order	ü	rule	ŦH	then		o in lemon
ėr	term					zh	measure		u in circus

B

ban·dit (ban′dit), a robber or thief, especially one of a gang of outlaws. *noun.*

bas·si·net or **bas·si·nette** (bas′n et′), a baby's basketlike cradle, usually with a hood over one end. *noun.*

box elder, a North American maple tree, often grown for shade or ornament.

broad (brôd), wide; large across: *Many cars can go on that broad, new road.* *adjective.*

bur·row (bėr′ō), **1** hole dug in the ground by an animal. Rabbits live in burrows. **2** dig a hole in the ground: *The mole quickly burrowed out of sight.* **1** *noun,* **2** *verb.*

C

cat·a·log (kat′l ôg), a list. A library usually has a catalog of its books, arranged in alphabetical order. Some companies print catalogs showing pictures and prices of the things that they have to sell. *noun.*

cau·tious (kô′shəs), very careful; not taking chances: *A cautious driver never drives too fast.* *adjective.*
—**cau′tious·ly,** *adverb.*

cel·lar (sel′ər), underground room or rooms, usually under a building and often used for storing food or fuel. *noun.*

cer·e·mo·ni·al (ser′ə mō′nē əl), of or having something to do with ceremony: *ceremonial costumes.* *adjective.*

cer·e·mo·ny (ser′ə mō′nē), **1** a special act or set of acts to be done on special occasions such as weddings, funerals, etc. **2** way of conducting oneself that follows all the rules for a certain occasion. *noun, plural* **cer·e·mo·nies.**

chal·lenge (chal′ənj), **1** invitation to a game or contest. **2** invite to a game or contest; dare: *They challenged our swimming team to beat their team.* **3** anything that claims or commands effort, interest, or feeling: *Fractions are a real challenge to me.* 1,3 *noun,* 2 *verb,* **chal·lenged, chal·leng·ing.**

cir·cum·stance (sėr′kəm stans), **1** condition that accompanies an act or event: *What were the circumstances that made you change your mind?* **2** fact or event: *It was a lucky circumstance that she found her money. noun.*
under no circumstances, never: *Under no circumstances should we tell anyone about our plans for the surprise party.*

coax (kōks), persuade by soft words; draw, get, or gain by means of gentle urging: *She coaxed me into letting her use my bike. verb.*

con·struc·tion (kən struk′shən), **1** act of constructing; building; putting together: *The construction of the bridge took nearly a month.* **2** thing built or put together: *The dolls' house was a construction of wood and cardboard. noun.*

con·ta·gious (kən tā′jəs), **1** catching; spreading by contact: *Mumps is a contagious disease.* **2** easily spreading from one to another. *adjective.*

con·tent (kən tent′), satisfied; contented; easy in mind: *Will you be content to wait till tomorrow? adjective.*

con·trap·tion (kən trap′shən), INFORMAL. device or gadget. *noun.*

crea·ture (krē′chər), any living person or animal: *We fed the lost dog because the poor creature was starving. noun.*

D

des·per·ate (des′pər it), **1** not caring what happens because hope is gone. **2** ready to try anything; ready to run any risk: *The team was desperate to win a game.* **3** having little chance for hope or cure; very dangerous: *a desperate illness. adjective.* —**des′per·ate·ly,** *adverb.*

dig·ni·fied (dig′nə fīd), having a formal manner; noble; stately: *The queen has a dignified manner. adjective.*

di·rec·tor (də rek′tər), manager; person who directs. A person who directs the performance of a play, a motion picture, or a show on television or radio is called a director. *noun.*

dis·ap·point·ment (dis′ə point′mənt), the feeling you have when you do not get what you expected or hoped for: *When she did not get a new bicycle, her disappointment was very great. noun.*

dis·taff (dis′taf), **1** a stick, split at the tip, to hold wool or flax for spinning by hand. **2** staff on a spinning wheel for holding wool or flax. *noun.*

doubt (dout), **1** not believe; not be sure; feel uncertain: *She doubted if we would arrive on time.* **2** an uncertain state of mind; a question about something or someone: *We were in doubt as to the right road.* 1 *verb,* 2 *noun.*

E

ed·u·ca·tion (ej′ə kā′shən),
1 training; schooling: *In the United States, public schools offer an education to all children.*
2 knowledge and abilities gained through training. *noun.* [*Education* comes from a Latin word meaning "a bringing up" or "a leading out."]

en·gi·neer·ing (en′jə nir′ing),
science of planning and building engines, machines, roads, bridges, canals, and the like. *noun.*

en·quire (en kwīr′), inquire. *verb,* **en·quired, en·quir·ing.**

ex·plo·sion (ek splō′zhən), **1** a blowing up; a bursting with a loud noise: *The explosion of the bomb shook the whole neighborhood.* **2** a loud noise caused by this: *People five miles away heard the explosion. noun.*

F

fas·ten (fas′n), tie, lock, or make hold together in any way: *fasten a door, fasten a seat belt. verb.*

fer·ry (fer′ē), **1** carry (people, vehicles, and goods) across a river or narrow stretch of water. **2** boat that makes the trip; ferryboat. **3** go across in a ferryboat. 1,3 *verb,* **fer·ried, fer·ry·ing;** 2 *noun,* *plural* **fer·ries.**

fra·grant (frā′grənt), having or giving off a pleasing odor; sweet-smelling: *Fragrant roses perfumed the air. adjective.*

fric·as·see (frik′ə sē′), **1** meat cut up, stewed, and served in a sauce made with its own gravy, *noun.*

fright·ful (frīt′fəl), **1** dreadful; terrible: *a frightful experience.* **2** INFORMAL. very great: *I'm in a frightful hurry. adjective.*
—fright′ful·ly, *adverb.*

a hat	**i** it	**oi** oil	**ch** child	**ə** stands for:	
ā age	**ī** ice	**ou** out	**ng** long	a in about	
ä far	**o** hot	**u** cup	**sh** she	e in taken	
e let	**ō** open	**ù** put	**th** thin	i in pencil	
ē equal	**ô** order	**ü** rule	**ŦH** then	o in lemon	
ėr term			**zh** measure	u in circus	

fum·ble (fum′bəl), **1** to search awkwardly; feel or grope around clumsily: *I fumbled in the darkness for the doorknob.* **2** to handle awkwardly; let drop instead of catching and holding: *The quarterback fumbled the ball, and the other team recovered it. verb,* **fum·bles, fum·bled, fum·bling.**

G

ga·losh·es (gə losh′iz), rubber or plastic overshoes covering the ankles, worn in wet or snowy weather. *noun, plural.*

ge·og·ra·phy (jē og′rə fē), study of the earth's surface, climate, continents, countries, peoples, industries, and products. *noun, plural* **ge·og·ra·phies.**

gnaw (nô), to bite at and wear away: *A mouse has gnawed right through the cover of this box. verb.*

grain (grān), **1** the seed of wheat, oats, corn, and other cereal grasses. **2** the smallest possible amount; tiniest bit. *noun.*

guar·an·tee (gar′ən tē′), **1** promise to pay or do something if another fails to do it; pledge to replace goods if they are not as represented: *We have a one-year guarantee on our new car.* **2** stand back of; give a guarantee for: *This company guarantees its clocks for a year.* 1 *noun,* 2 *verb,* **guar·an·teed, guar·an·tee·ing.**

H

har·ness (här′nis), **1** leather straps, bands, and other pieces for a horse, which connect it to a carriage, wagon, or plow, or are used in riding. Reins, collar, and bridle are parts of a horse's harness. **2** put harness on: *Harness the horse.* **1** *noun, plural* **har·ness·es;** **2** *verb.*

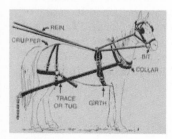

harness

hedge (hej), **1** a thick row of bushes or small trees planted as a fence. *noun.*

hol·ly·hock (hol′ē hok), a tall plant with clusters of large, showy flowers of various colors. *noun.*

hu·man (hyü′mən), of or having the form or qualities of people: *Men, women, and children are human beings. Those monkeys seem almost human. adjective.* [*Human* comes from a Latin word meaning "of man" or "of human beings."]

hu·mil·i·ate (hyü mil′ē āt), lower the pride, dignity, or self-respect of: *We felt humiliated by our failure. They humiliated me by criticizing me in front of my friends. verb,* **hu·mil·i·at·ed, hu·mil·i·at·ing.**

I

ig·nore (ig nôr′), pay no attention to; disregard: *The driver ignored the traffic light and almost hit another car. verb,* **ig·nored, ig·nor·ing.**

im·i·tate (im′ə tāt), **1** copy; make or do something like: *A parrot imitates the sounds it hears.* **2** act like: *He amused the class by imitating a duck, a monkey, and a bear. verb,* **im·i·tat·ed, im·i·tat·ing.**

im·i·ta·tion (im′ə tā′shən), **1** imitating: *We learn many things by imitation.* **2** copy: *Give as good an imitation as you can of a rooster crowing. noun.*

in·dig·nant (in dig′nənt), angry at something unworthy, unfair, or mean. *adjective.* —**in·dig′nant·ly,** *adverb.*

indignant—He was very **indignant** when I told him I didn't like his hair.

in·flam·ma·tion (in′flə mā′shən), a diseased condition of some part of the body, marked by heat, redness, swelling, and pain: *A boil is an inflammation of the skin. noun.*

in·quire (in kwīr′), **1** try to find out by questions; ask: *The detective went from house to house, inquiring if anyone had seen anything suspicious.* **2** make a search for information, knowledge, or truth: *The man read many old documents while inquiring into the history of the town. verb,* **in·quired, in·quir·ing.**

in·sult (in sult′ *for 1;* in′sult *for 2*),
1 say or do something very scornful,
rude, or harsh to: *She insulted me
by calling me a liar.* **2** an insulting
speech or action: *It is an insult to
call someone stupid.* 1 *verb,* 2 *noun.*

in·tel·li·gent (in tel′ə jənt), having
or showing understanding; able to
learn and know; quick at learning:
Elephants are intelligent animals.
adjective.

a hat	**i** it	**oi** oil	**ch** child	**ə** stands for:
ā age	**ī** ice	**ou** out	**ng** long	a in about
ä far	**o** hot	**u** cup	**sh** she	e in taken
e let	**ō** open	**ù** put	**th** thin	i in pencil
ē equal	**ô** order	**ü** rule	**ŦH** then	o in lemon
ėr term			**zh** measure	u in circus

J

joy (joi), **1** happiness; glad feeling:
*She jumped for joy when she saw
the circus.* **2** something that causes
gladness or happiness: *On a hot
day, a cool swim is a joy. noun.*

K

keen (kēn), **1** finely sharpened so as
to cut well: *a keen blade.* **2** sharp;
cutting: *a keen wind, keen pain,
keen wit. adjective.*

L

lac·quer (lak′ər), **1** varnish used to
give a coating or a shiny appear-
ance to metals, wood, or paper. **2**
coat with lacquer. 1 *noun,* 2 *verb.*

las·so (las′ō), **1** a long rope with a
loop at the end for catching horses
and cattle; lariat. **2** catch with a
lasso. 1 *noun,* 2 *verb*

leek (lēk), vegetable somewhat like a
long, thick, green onion. *noun.*

lob·by (lob′ē), entrance hall;
passageway: *the lobby of a theater,
a hotel lobby. noun, plural*
lob·bies.

lyr·ics (lir′iks), the words for a song.
noun.

M

marsh (märsh), low land covered at
times by water; soft, wet land;
swamp. *noun, plural* **marsh·es.**

mas·to·don (mas′tə don), any of a
large group of extinct animals much
like mammoths and present-day
elephants. *noun.*

maternity ward, part of a hospital
designed for the care of newborn
babies and their mothers.

men·tion (men′shən), **1** speak
about: *I mentioned your idea to the
group that is planning the picnic.*
2 a short statement; a reference to:
*There was mention of our school
party in the newspaper.* 1 *verb,*
2 *noun.*

me·squite (me skēt′), a tree or
shrub common in the southwestern
United States and Mexico. Mesquite
often grows in dense clumps or
thickets and bears pods that are
used as food for cattle. *noun.*

meth·od (meth′əd), **1** way of doing
something: *a method of teaching
music.* **2** order or system for getting
things done. *noun.*

mim·ic (mim′ik), **1** make fun of by
imitating. **2** person or thing that
imitates. **3** copy closely; imitate: *A
parrot can mimic voices.* 1,3 *verb,*
mim·icked, mim·ick·ing;
2 *noun.*

mul·ber·ry (mul′ber′ē), tree with
small berrylike fruit that can be
eaten. *noun, plural* **mul·ber·ries.**

myr·tle (mėr′tl), an evergreen shrub
of the southern part of Europe, with
shiny leaves and fragrant white
flowers.

N

nat·ur·al (nach′ər əl), **1** produced by nature; coming in the ordinary course of events: *natural feelings and actions.* **2** belonging to the nature one is born with: *It is natural for ducks to swim. adjective.*

nec·tar (nek′tər), **1** (in ancient Greek stories) the drink of the gods. **2** a sweet liquid found in many flowers. Bees gather nectar and make it into honey. *noun.*

nes·tle (nes′əl), settle oneself comfortably or cozily: *She nestled down into the big chair. verb,* **nes·tled, nes·tling.**

noc·tur·nal (nok tér′nl), **1** of the night: *Stars are a nocturnal sight.* **2** in the night: *a nocturnal visitor.* **3** active in the night: *The owl is a nocturnal bird. adjective.*

O

o·blige (ə blīj′), **1** bind by a promise; compel; force: *The law obliges parents to send their children to school.* **2** put under a debt of thanks for some favor or service: *We are very much obliged for your kind offer. verb,* **o·bliged, o·blig·ing.**

much obliged, a commonly used phrase to express thanks.

or·di·nar·y (ôrd′n er′ē), **1** according to habit or custom; usual; regular; normal: *an ordinary day's work.* **2** not special; common; everyday; average: *an ordinary person, an ordinary situation. adjective.*

P

pan·ic (pan′ik), **1** sudden uncontrollable fear that causes a person or group to lose self-control;

unreasoning fear: *When the theater caught fire, there was a panic.* **2** to be affected with panic: *The audience panicked when the fire broke out.* **1** *noun,* **2** *verb,* **pan·ics, pan·icked, pan·ick·ing.**

par·lor (pär′lər), **1** room for receiving or entertaining guests; sitting room. **2** a decorated room used as a shop: *a beauty parlor. noun.*

pass (pas), **1** go by; move past: *The parade passed. We passed a truck.* **2** a narrow road, path, or opening: *A pass crosses the mountains.* **1** *verb,* **2** *noun.*

pe·cul·iar (pi kyü′lyər), strange; odd; unusual: *A clock with no hands looks peculiar. adjective.*

pel·let (pel′lit), a little ball of mud, paper, fur, hail, snow, food, or medicine. *noun.*

per·cent (pər sent′), **1** parts in each hundred; hundredths. 5 percent is 5 of each 100, or 5/100 of the whole. **2** part; proportion: *A large percent of the state's apple crop was ruined. noun.*

per cent, See percent.

pli·ers (plī′ərz), small pincers with long jaws for bending or cutting wire or holding small objects. *noun plural or singular.*

pliers

pre·cise (pri sīs′), **1** correct; exact; accurate: *The directions they gave were so precise that we found our way easily.* **2** very careful: *She is precise in her work. adjective.*
—**pre·cise′ly,** *adverb.*

pre·his·to·ric (prē′hi stôr′ik), of or belonging to times before histories were written: *Prehistoric peoples used stone tools. adjective.*

a	hat	i	it	oi	oil	ch	child	ə	stands for:
ā	age	ī	ice	ou	out	ng	long		a in about
ä	far	o	hot	u	cup	sh	she		e in taken
e	let	ō	open	ů	put	th	thin		i in pencil
ē	equal	ô	order	ü	rule	ŦH	then		o in lemon
ėr	term					zh	measure		u in circus

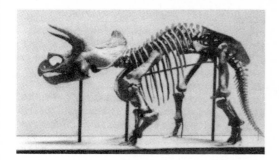

prehistoric—the skeleton of a **prehistoric** animal

pre·scrip·tion (pri skrip′shən), a written direction or order for preparing and using a medicine: *a prescription for a cough. noun.*

Q

quail (kwāl), a plump, wild bird that is hunted and used for food. A bobwhite is one kind of quail. *noun, plural* **quails** *or* **quail.**

quar·tet (kwôr tet′), **1** group of four singers or players performing together. **2** any group of four. *noun.*

R

rea·son·a·ble (rē′zn ə bəl), **1** according to reason; sensible; not foolish: *When we are angry, we do not always act in a reasonable way.* **2** not asking too much; fair; just: *a reasonable person. adjective.*

re·flect (ri flekt′), turn back or throw back (light, heat, sound, or the like): *The sidewalks reflect heat on a hot day. verb.*

re·hears·al (ri hėr′səl), a practice for a public performance of a play, concert, *etc. noun.*

rel·a·tive (rel′ə tiv), **1** person who belongs to the same family as another, such as a father, brother, aunt, nephew, or cousin. **2** an animal or plant related to another by common descent. *noun.*

re·tire (ri tīr′), **1** give up an office or occupation: *Our teachers retire at 65.* **2** go to bed: *We retire early. verb,* **re·tired, re·tir·ing.**

ro·dent (rōd′nt), any of a group of animals with four large front teeth that they often use to gnaw wood. Rats, mice, and squirrels are rodents. *noun.*

rodent—Hamsters are **rodents.**

S

sa·ber-toothed ti·ger (sā′bər tütht′ tī′gər), a large, prehistoric mammal somewhat like a tiger. Its upper canine teeth were very long and curved.

saber-toothed tiger—about 7 ft. (2 m.) long with the tail

sat·is·fac·tion (sat′i sfak′shən), **1** condition of being pleased and contented: *She felt satisfaction at having done well.* **2** anything that makes us feel pleased or contented: *It is a great satisfaction to have things turn out just the way you want. noun.*

se·date (si dāt′), quiet; calm; serious: *I was very sedate as a child and often preferred reading to playing. adjective.* —**se·date′ly,** *adverb.*

shield (shēld), **1** piece of armor carried on the arm to protect the body in battle. **2** anything used to protect: *I turned up my collar as a shield against the cold wind.* **3** protect; defend: *They shielded me from unjust punishment.* 1,2 *noun,* 3 *verb.*

stern (stèrn), severe; strict; harsh: *Our teacher's stern frown silenced us. adjective.* —**stern′ly,** *adverb.*

steth·o·scope (steth′ə skōp), instrument used by doctors when listening to sounds in the lungs, heart, or other part of the body. *noun.*

stub·ble (stub′əl), the lower ends of stalks of grain left in the ground after the grain is cut: *The stubble hurt her bare feet. noun.*

sur·face (sèr′fis), **1** the outside of anything: *the surface of a mountain.* **2** any face or side of a thing: *A cube has six surfaces. The upper surface of the plate has pictures on it. noun.*

sus·pect (sə spekt′), **1** imagine to be so; think lively: *The old fox suspected danger and did not touch the trap.* **2** believe guilty, false, or bad without proof: *The police suspected them of being thieves. verb.*

sus·pi·cious (sə spish′əs), **1** causing one to suspect: *Someone suspicious was hanging around the house.* **2** feeling suspicion; suspecting: *Our dog is suspicious of strangers. adjective.*

syc·a·more (sik′ə môr), kind of shade tree with large leaves and light-colored bark that peels off in tiny scales. *noun.*

sym·pa·thet·i·cal·ly (sim′pə thet′ik lē), in a tender, gentle, friendly way; with kindness: *The doctor spoke sympathetically while he bandaged my leg. adverb.*

sym·pa·thy (sim′pə thē), sharing another's sorrow or trouble: *We feel sympathy for a person who is ill. noun, plural* **sym·pa·thies.**

T

te·di·ous (tē′dē əs *or* tē′jəs), long and tiring: *A talk that you cannot understand is tedious. adjective.*

trol·ley (trol′ē), pulley at the end of a pole that moves against a wire to carry electricity to a streetcar or an electric engine. A **trolley car** or **trolley bus** is a streetcar or bus having such a pulley. *noun, plural* **trol·leys.**

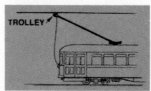

trolley car

trough (trôf), **1** a long, narrow container for holding food or water: *We led our horses to the watering trough.* **2** something shaped like this. **3** a long hollow between two ridges, etc.: *the trough between two waves. noun.*

tu·nic (tü′nik, tyü′nik), **1** garment like a shirt or gown worn by men and women in ancient Greece and Rome. **2** any garment like this. **3** a woman's garment, usually belted, extending below the waist or over the skirt. *noun.*

tur·nip (tèr′nəp), the large, fleshy, roundish root of a garden plant, eaten as a vegetable. *noun.*

a hat	**i** it	**oi** oil	**ch** child	**ə** stands for:
ā age	**ī** ice	**ou** out	**ng** long	a in about
ä far	**o** hot	**u** cup	**sh** she	e in taken
e let	**ō** open	**ù** put	**th** thin	i in pencil
ē equal	**ô** order	**ü** rule	**ŦH** then	o in lemon
ėr term			**zh** measure	u in circus

U

un·cer·tain·ty (un sèrt′n tē), uncertain state; doubt. *noun.*

un·con·scious (un kon′shəs), **1** not able to feel; not awake: *He was knocked unconscious by the blow.* **2** not aware: *Unconscious of the time, she kept on reading and missed her piano lesson. adjective.*

un·der·tone (un′dər tōn′), a low or very quiet tone: *talk in undertones. noun.*

V

vel·vet (vel′vit), **1** a soft cloth with short raised threads on one side. **2** like velvet: *Our cat has velvet paws.* 1 *noun,* 2 *adjective.*

W

wail (wāl), **1** cry loud and long because of grief or pain: *The baby wailed.* **2** a long cry of grief or pain. **3** a sound like such a cry: *the wail of a hungry coyote.* 1 *verb,* 2,3 *noun.*

web (web), **1** a woven net of very tiny threads like silk spun by a spider. **2** a whole piece of cloth made at one time. **3** anything like a web: *a web of lies.* **4** the skin joining the toes of swimming birds such as ducks and of other water animals such as frogs and beavers. *noun.*

webbed (webd), having the toes joined by a web. Ducks have webbed feet. *adjective.*

won·drous (wun′drəs), wonderful. *adjective.*

X

X ray, 1 a ray which can go through substances that rays of light cannot penetrate. X rays are used to locate breaks in bones or decay in teeth, and to treat certain diseases. **2** a photograph made by means of X rays.

Y

yip (yip), INFORMAL. **1** (especially of dogs) bark or yelp briskly. **2** a sharp, barking sound. 1 *verb,* **yipped, yip·ping;** 2 *noun.*

Z

zip (zip), **1** fasten or close with a zipper: *zip up one's jacket.* **2** INFORMAL. proceed with energy; go fast. *verb,* **zipped, zip·ping.**

Word List

The following words all appear in the glossary. Those followed by an asterisk are introduced optionally in the Teacher's Edition.

Ramona Forever
bassinette
contagious*
disappointment*
humiliate
inflammation*
lobby*
maternity ward
prescription*
stethoscope
sympathy

Anna, Grandpa, and the Big Storm
abruptly
cautiously*
circumstance
galoshes*
harness
indignantly
parlor*
shield
sternly*
trolley car*

A Grain of Wheat
box elder
education*
engineering
explosion*
geography*
grain*
hedge
hollyhock
mulberry
sycamore*

Thumbeline
broad*
distaff*
ferry*
fragrant
lacquer
myrtle
nectar*
stubble
tedious*
unconscious

The Stories Julian Tells
catalog*
fasten
mastodon
method*
ordinary*
pliers
prehistoric*
reflect*
saber-toothed
    tiger
satisfaction

The Rooster Who Understood Japanese
altar
ceremonial*
coax
dignified*
fricassee
intelligent*
mimic
natural*
retire
sympathetic*

Amigo
burrow*
content*
creature
human
mesquite*
nestle*
pass*
quail
surface
wail

Hear the Music
audition*
cellar
director*
lasso
lyrics*
quartet*
rehearsal*
velvet

From Anna
alcove
challenge*
desperately*
fumble
panic
sedate*
trough*
tunic*
uncertainty
undertone

The Sneetches
contraption*
doubt
frightful
guarantee*
keen*
peculiar*
per cent
precise*
wondrous
zip

**Animal Tracks and
Wildlife Signs**
attract
bandit
construction*
gnaw*
marsh*
nocturnal*
pellet
relative
rodent*
webbed

Clancy's Coat
admit*
annoy*
enquire
ignore
insult*
leek*
mention
oblige
reasonable*
turnip